THE BOY SOLDIER

BOY SOLDIER

Edwin Jemison and the Story Behind
the Most Remarkable Portrait of the Civil War

Alexandra Filipowski

Hugh T. Harrington

WESTHOLME
Yardley

Facing title page: Private Edwin Francis Jemison, 2nd Louisiana Volunteer Regiment. (*Library of Congress, from a daguerreotype owned by Jemison's descendants*)

Westholme Publishing, LLC
904 Edgewood Road
Yardley, Pennsylvania 19067
Visit our Web site at www.westholmepublishing.com

First Printing October 2016
ISBN: 978-1-59416-264-0
Also available as an eBook.

Printed in the United States of America

For my father, George, who introduced me to the
 Civil War,
my mother Daphne, who encouraged me to find out
 more,
and my husband Scott, who has always supported me

—AF

To Sue for her decades of patience and support

—HTH

With gratitude to all American service men and women:
past, present, and future

—AF and HTH

CONTENTS

List of Illustrations

FOREWORD

Mark H. Dunkelman

The development and immediate popularity of photography following the 1839 introduction of the daguerreotype brought portraiture within reach of the masses for the first time in human history. As photographic historian Bob Zeller has observed, "In a phenomenally short period of time, photographers, their gear, and studios became as familiar on the American landscape as blacksmiths or a team of mules." When the Civil War erupted, roughly fifteen hundred photographers were at work in North and South. Historian William C. Davis estimates they most likely produced more than one million images during the conflict, "the overwhelming majority of them portraits of individual soldiers."

Whenever they had the means and opportunity, Civil War volunteers sat for their "likenesses," as mid-nineteenth-century Americans often termed photographs. Frequently these portraits were taken when newly recruited regiments were organizing at local camps before traveling to the front.

Throughout the war, itinerant photographers set up makeshift studios at army encampments far and wide and took many other soldier portraits. In virtually all of the cases, the photographs were given or sent to the subject's family or friends, as mementoes of their absent loved ones. Treasured as such, they became priceless relics when the soldiers they pictured never returned home, having died in the service from a multitude of causes.

Edwin Jemison was one of the hundreds of thousands of Civil War soldiers who sat for a photographic portrait to give to his family. Like many of those portraits, Jemison's would have remained a private possession, concealed in an album or curio cabinet in the home of a relative, had it not been reproduced in *The American Heritage Picture History of the Civil War*. This popular 1960 publication included a full-page copy of the Jemison daguerreotype over the caption, "A haunting face from a truly lost generation: Georgia private Edwin Jennison, killed at Malvern Hill."

The American Heritage book brought the evocative face to a wide audience, including this writer, then a twelve-year-old with a growing interest in Civil War history. Among the many others struck by the poignant image was a New Hampshire teacher, Jo-Ann Aiello, whose curiosity about the boy in the picture led her to discover that the book's caption had incorrectly stated his surname and the state from which he served. Aiello's work cleared up the misidentification, but much remained to be learned about young Edwin Jemison.

Enter Alexandra Filipowski, another person captivated by the Jemison portrait. While still living in her hometown of New York City, in the 1990s she began to research the Jemison family in depth. Her discoveries led her to Milledgeville, Georgia, and—inevitably—Hugh T. Harrington, the most dedicated chronicler of that city's history. Together, the two of them dug deeply in historical records to extract the story of the boy in what has become one of the iconic images of the Civil War.

Filipowski and Harrington have done what they set out to do—they have freed Edwin Jemison from the matted daguerreotype and followed him as his path led from Georgia to Louisiana to the battlefields of Virginia, and to his ultimate fate on the slopes of Malvern Hill. Thanks to their diligent work, Edwin Jemison now has two haunting portraits—one in a photograph, the other in the words of this book.

INTRODUCTION

On a hot New Orleans day in May 1861 a young man, a boy really, looked into the lens of the daguerreotype camera as the photographer captured his image. The young man was sixteen-year-old Edwin F. Jemison of Monroe, Louisiana, the youngest member in the Pelican Grays of the 2nd Louisiana Volunteer Infantry. Like countless soldiers on both sides of the Mason–Dixon Line, he was having his picture taken in uniform to send back home, to his family in Monroe. He could hardly have imagined that a hundred years later his image would become the icon of lost youth of the Civil War and, perhaps by extension, the lost youth of all wars: past, present, and future.

Since the image was first made public in 1960 with its inclusion in *The American Heritage Picture History of the Civil War*,[1] Eddie, as his family called him, has attracted and haunted people from around the world. No one knew, except

Eddie's family of course, that the young man in the daguerreotype had been misidentified as "Edwin Jennison" and recorded as a private from Georgia. Through the excellent research of Jo-Ann Aiello of Salem, New Hampshire, the man in the image was properly identified in the early 1990s. The quest that led Aiello to discover Eddie's true identity was prompted by her desire to know more about the boy behind the image. Aiello first became familiar with the photo as a teenager in the late 1960s, and she fell in love with his image.

Time moved on, but she never forgot his face. In 1979 she decided it was time to find out more about the soldier whose face she first gazed upon so many years before. She spent years searching, contacting institutions such as the National Archives and the Georgia Archives, but every lead was a dead end. Frustrated, she was nearly resigned to the fact that her quest was to end in failure. Strangely, she had a dream where Eddie appeared, looking impatient, and said "My home is Monroe." She soon found in the Library of Congress records that there was a soldier from Louisiana named "E. F. Jennison" who served in the 2nd Louisiana Infantry. She searched the handwritten 1860 census of Monroe, Louisiana, and found the name of a lawyer which could be either "Jennison" or "Jemison." The lawyer had a son whose initials were "E. F." She tracked the family and found it to be Jemison. The "m" had been misread as a double "n."

Aiello's journey did not end there. The definitive proof came when she tracked down a great-niece of E. F. Jemison's, who in turn invited Aeillo to visit her. It was during this visit that Aiello was shown the original daguerreotype of young Eddie. It was the same young man who had captivated her so long ago.[2]

Aiello submitted her findings to the Library of Congress and the National Park Service to correct their records and properly identify Edwin F. Jemison's service and his image. In 1991, the Library of Congress corrected their records. Jo-Ann Aiello's quest was successfully concluded.

On another hot day, this time in New York City in the 1980s, Alexandra Filipowski leafed through the pages of her father's copy of *The American Heritage Picture History of the Civil War*. It was then that she first saw Eddie's picture. Like Jo-Ann Aiello, she was drawn to the young man staring at her from the page. Alexandra was only ten years old at the time, but something about his face drew her in. Like Aiello, she tried to find out more about him, writing to the Georgia Archives, but came up empty-handed. And so she waited, impatiently. Beginning in the 1990s with the advent of the Internet, Alexandra would periodically search for "Edwin Jennison," knowing that someday something would come up.

In 1999, she discovered an article which had first appeared in the *Union Recorder*[3] several years before, reporting the story of Aiello's discovery of the correct identity of Eddie. Finally, Filipowski knew who he was. But she wanted to know more. She began to seek out information about who his family was and what happened to them. Through the *Union Recorder* article, Filipowski learned that Eddie and his family were buried at Memory Hill Cemetery in Milledgeville, Georgia. A search found the cemetery's web site, which included not only an index of graves, but also photographs. It was then that she first saw the site where Eddie was "buried." But was he really there? There was just one monument for both Eddie and his brother, Henry. Were they both there, she asked herself. Wanting to know, in the fall of 2001 she wrote to Sue Harrington, the president of Friends of Baldwin County Cemeteries and creator of the Memory Hill Cemetery web site, asking, "Is Private Jemison actually buried at Memory Hill, or is he really at Malvern Hill where he died?"

Sue Harrington's speciality was cemetery preservation and indexing cemeteries in central Georgia. When questions came to her involving history, she turned them over to her husband, Hugh.

In the 1960s Hugh Harrington had seen Eddie's image in the *American Heritage Picture History of the Civil War*. He had also seen, and saved, the article from the *Union Recorder*. In response to Alexandra Filipowski's request he went to the cemetery lot where the Jemison family was buried. He looked at the monuments, the dates of death, and particularly the obelisk bearing the names of both Henry Jemison and Edwin Jemison. When he returned home he sent a reply to Filipowski reporting what he found and his views on the possible burial of Edwin Jemison in the cemetery.

What started as a simple email request turned into a torrent of exchanged emails. Theories were advanced, discussed, dissected, and research progressed. Harrington found himself drawn into a quest for any and all information about Eddie Jemison. It was a quest that would go on for over fifteen years.

In the spring of 2002 the Harringtons did something very unusual. They invited Alexandra Filipowski, a New Yorker whom they did not know and had never even spoken to, not only to visit Milledgeville but to stay in their home. The resulting visit was astonishing. Filipowski displayed a vast knowledge, gleaned from countless hours at the New York Public Library, of not only the genealogy of mid-nineteenth-century families in central Georgia but also which families had business ties with each other.

Hugh Harrington and Alexandra Filipowski visited every location in Baldwin and Bibb counties with a connection to the Jemison family. A couple of hours were spent in the Stubbs house in Milledgeville, Georgia, where Eddie Jemison lived for three years with his maternal grandparents and several of his young aunts and uncles.[4] The house in 2002 was little changed from the 1850s. Together they walked the old floors, examined every room, even looking through the big keyhole in the old front door lock. They went into the two upstairs bedrooms that would have been a sort of dormitory for the children. This is where Eddie had lived and slept. For over one hundred years no one had known that he had lived here; now only two people knew. It was a magical moment; they spoke in whispers.

Together they trekked through cemeteries and old houses and were welcomed by current homeowners to hear tales of the land the Jemisons lived on, and in some cases, old family stories. If their combined love of history and interest in Eddie did not solidify their partnership in research, then the trip did.

Despite the fascination people have with Eddie and the longing to know more, little has been written about his life. Some people know the basics—that he was born into a well-to-do Georgia family in 1844, lived in Louisiana, and died a violent death on the battlefield of Malvern Hill on July 1, 1862. However, not much accurate information has been readily available, and entirely erroneous information is widespread.

Extensive research over many years in libraries and archives, interviews with family members, and fieldwork at various sites has enabled Eddie's life to emerge as never before. Utilizing new and never before seen materials Eddie's story is told in these pages. It is the story of the boy behind the image.

Chapter One

IN THE BEGINNING

Sarah Jemison stared at the picture. Her son, Eddie, stared back at her from the daguerreotype. It was the summer of 1862—in the midst of the Civil War. Eddie's face was sad, almost haunting, even though he was dressed in his uniform. Instead of downcast, he should have, after all, been proud and excited to join the Confederacy, she may have thought. He wanted badly to join, and she and her husband, Robert, likely reluctantly agreed that he could, despite his young age of sixteen.

But why did he look so sad? He had had a good childhood. He was born Edwin Francis Jemison on December 1, 1844, on his father's wooded plantation on Thomaston Road, eight miles northwest of Macon, Georgia. The family consisted of his parents, Robert and Sarah, and his elder brother, Henry (b. 1842). Another brother, Owen, followed two years later. In 1847 they began to plan their exodus from Georgia. The cotton industry was flourishing in Louisiana and opportunities presented themselves there.[1] Sarah's brother, Frank Stubbs, who had just turned seventeen that September and was about to graduate from Oglethorpe University, would join them in what was thought to be a great new adventure in Louisiana.[2]

Beginning in October 1847, Robert began to advertise that the auction of his property was to take place on November 22, if it had not already been sold by that time. The auction included all his stock, crops, equipment, and household goods and furniture.[3] They were selling almost everything to start a new life in Louisiana.

In late 1847 Eddie, along with his father, mother (who was pregnant),[4] his brothers, and his Uncle Frank Stubbs settled in northern Louisiana. Frank became a school teacher in Ouachita Parish, while Eddie and his family settled in Jackson Parish.[5] Jackson Parish is located in the central part of northern Louisiana, an area heavily wooded in pine trees. Once cleared, the land would produce cotton.

Robert took advantage of the inexpensive, fertile soil and purchased his first piece of property in January 1848.[6] He continued buying land and in November 1850 his real estate was valued at $4,000. In the first thirteen years the family accumulated 1,354.91 acres, mostly in Jackson Parish, with a small portion of adjoining land in Ouachita Parish. By 1860 the real estate value had grown to $30,000 and personal estate valued at $3,000. Robert had also owned a total of twenty-nine slaves.[7]

Eddie had spent his early years playing with his brothers Henry, Owen, and Robert, Jr. (b. 1847). They were later joined by another brother, Samuel (b. 1852). Sarah would have raised her boys and run her home much the way a cap-

Robert Jemison, Sr., Edwin's father.
(*John and Elaine Stallard*)

Sarah Stubbs Jemison, Edwin's mother.
(*John and Elaine Stallard*)

tain would run his ship, with great care and efficiency. The management of a plantation home was a demanding job. Doing laundry alone consisted of boiling vast amounts of water, scrubbing of clothes and linens, rinsing, and hanging them to dry. It was an all-day endeavor, just like most household chores of the time. Baking bread, washing dishes, plucking chickens for Sunday dinner all took time and people.

She and her husband Robert had tried to raise their children well and give them the education to help them be successful, like Robert, who was an attorney. In the summer of 1857 they sent Eddie and Henry to live with her parents, Baradell and Eliza Stubbs, in Midway, Georgia, so that they could pursue a more formal education.[8] It was the first time that Eddie and Henry—now aged twelve and fourteen—would venture away from home. There was great hustle and bustle at the Jemison plantation in Louisiana. Trunks and bags were being packed, travel arrangements made, and good-byes were said.

The Stubbs lived in the clapboard plantation-style house where Sarah had grown up. She was the eldest of eleven children.[9] The house was not large considering the number of people who lived there: four rooms on the lower floor divided by a central hall forming two living areas that could be used as a dining room and parlor, a bedroom for Baradell and Eliza, and a kitchen. An old windowpane in the kitchen bears the crude etching "RNS," a memento from the hand of Richard Nichols Stubbs, Sarah's younger brother.[10]

In the kitchen was a stairway that led to a landing on the second floor. To each side of the landing was a door that led to two large attic rooms, one side for the boys and one side for the girls. As a girl Sarah had lived up there. With all the giggling and playfulness it is a wonder that they got any sleep.[11]

The Stubbs's household was large, even as grandsons Eddie and Henry moved in. Besides Baradell and Eliza, six younger people called that house their home. There were four Stubbs daughters, aunts of Eddie and Henry: eleven-year-old Emma, fourteen-year-old Ellen, twenty-year-old Louisa, and twenty-four-year-old Catherine. Also there were two sons, uncles to the Jemison boys: eight-year-old Richard and seventeen-year-old Willie.[12] Due to their ages, and that they all lived in the same house, the Stubbs aunts and uncles were much more like brothers and sisters rather than traditional aunts and uncles to the Jemison boys. Nearby there were two more aunts, Martha Stubbs Small and Julia Stubbs Pratt, living with their husbands. Other relations, of various degrees of closeness, were within a few miles.

Baradell Stubbs was a pillar of the community. Besides being a plantation owner he was a justice of the peace and a member of the executive committee of the Presbyterian Education Society. The society had first opened Midway Seminary/Midway Male Academy in 1834 as a manual labor school. When, a year later, it was decided that a collegiate level of education was needed, they opened Oglethorpe University and kept the academy as its preparatory school. Eddie's father, Robert, was enrolled at Oglethorpe University the first year it opened and was part of its second graduating class. Besides their father, they had four cousins, three uncles, and an uncle-by-marriage who were all Oglethorpe graduates. A cousin and another uncle were currently enrolled. An additional two cousins and another uncle would be attending Midway Male Academy with Eddie and Henry.

The Midway Male Academy was next-door to the Stubbs's home in Midway. While the academy was a very modest two-room frame building, it was home to a rigorous teaching regimen.[13] The academy required the boys to learn Latin and Greek with the intent of being able to compose in those languages, as well as read, analyze texts, and study rhetoric and oratory.[14] Eddie and Henry along with their seven-year-old uncle Richard Stubbs left the Stubbs's house for their first day of this rather intimidating school.

When Eddie, Henry, and Richard reached the school,

Baradell P. Stubbs, Edwin's maternal grandfather.

Stubbs's house, Midway, Georgia. (*Hugh T. Harrington*)

they were joined by thirty other boys, including their cousins Charles and John Hammond.[15] At seventeen, Charles may have been a little too old to be a playmate for Eddie and Henry, although there can be little doubt that they spent time together as a family, but John, who had just turned fourteen, was the perfect age for Eddie and Henry to have as a companion.

While Eddie was in Midway attending school in May 1859 he saw death up close. An old man was lying white and cold on the cooling board in the parlor of his home. The room and the house were draped with black mourning crepe.[16] This was no ordinary man who lay there. Family and the closest of friends were milling about, speaking in hushed tones. To fourteen-year-old Eddie it would be a transforming experience. He had not known his great-uncle Dr. Tomlinson Fort[17] well. He had seen him only on occasion for the last year or so at various family gatherings or when Eddie would call at the Fort house on Greene Street to play with his cousins. Those cousins were in attendance this day, along with many others. They would soon be joined by what seemed like all of Milledgeville, everyone wishing to pay their last respects to a man all regarded so highly.

Eddie would have almost certainly known in a vague sort of way of Dr. Fort's illustrious career. He was not only a highly esteemed physician and author of a medical book, *A Dissertation on the Practice of Medicine*, he had also served in the Georgia state legislature, was a three-term mayor of Milledgeville, and was instrumental in the establishment of the Georgia Lunatic Asylum. In addition, he was a trustee of the University of Georgia, served in the United States Congress, and founded the local *Federal Union* newspaper.

However, Eddie would not have been really interested in most of these accomplishments. They were all beyond his understanding. What was within his youthful comprehension was Dr. Fort's heroics in the military. He had, of course, heard stories and had even heard old Dr. Fort speak of some of those adventures within the family. This day, as he wandered unnoticed among the men at Fort's house, he heard them speak of those tales yet again, softly and reverently in the presence of death. More than one mourner would have recalled the 1812 Battle of Twelve Mile Swamp. Very likely the young boy listened intently to the dramatic tale.

The story of the Battle (skirmish, really) of Twelve Mile Swamp was memorable and one that would have struck a chord with almost any young teenage boy. Perhaps this story would resonate with this boy to a degree that it would affect his future life choices. Dr. Fort would provide a role model that would be hard to ignore.

In 1812, twenty-five-year-old Tomlinson Fort formed his own militia company to fight in the little known "Patriot War" in Florida.[18] On September 12, 1812, Captain Tomlinson Fort was ordered to accompany a detachment of U.S. Marines escorting two supply wagons from Fort Mose, near St. Augustine, to the supply depot at the blockhouse at Davis Creek (now Bayard, Florida) about twenty miles to the northwest. The escort consisted of a corporal, nineteen privates, two wagon drivers, and Fort, all under the command of Marine Corps captain John Williams.

The route the wagons followed (modern U.S. Route 1) was called the "King's Road," a narrow, rough, and overgrown path. The road passed through Twelve Mile Swamp,[19] a morass of cypress bogs and palmetto thickets. It was with darkness falling that the small caravan entered the dismal, forbidding swamp where visibility was reduced to mere feet. Between 8 and 9 p.m. a volley was fired from out of the surrounding undergrowth from both sides of the road. The party of Americans had been ambushed by a force of fifty to sixty blacks and Seminole Indians.

Captain Williams attempted to rally his men into a defensive position when a second volley burst from the darkness. Williams went down, wounded. Captain Fort ran to his side and began dragging Williams to the scanty cover available.

Dr. Tomlinson Fort, Edwin's great uncle. (*James C. Bonner Collection, Special Collections, Georgia College Library, Milledgeville, Georgia*)

Tomlinson Fort burial monument. (*Hugh T. Harrington*)

Enemy balls again and again found their mark in Williams's body. The corporal, fighting nearby, received a mortal wound. The musket ball that pierced the corporal's body went through and lodged in Fort's knee. Fort grabbed the corporal's musket and fought back. With the Marine officer out of action Fort assumed command.

The Marines, under the leadership of Captain Fort, regrouped and fought doggedly. The fighting was desperate and at very close quarters. Both sides were shooting at muzzle flashes, movement in the brush, Indian war whoops, and other noises. Having used up most of their ammunition, Fort and his men lay in the swamp behind their bayonets, peering into the darkness for hours, not knowing whether another attack might come in a rush. The enemy silently withdrew sometime that night, evidently satisfied with the burning of one wagon and the taking of another. The following day Fort and his men were rescued by a relief force from the blockhouse.

Captain John Williams, wounded eight times, survived for seventeen days before expiring. The corporal, scalped within full view of his comrades, was the only other fatality. Seven privates were wounded, as was Tomlinson Fort.

The musket ball that entered Captain Fort's knee could not be removed. It remained there and gave him great pain, along with an accompanying limp, for the next forty years. Eventually, the pain was such that Dr. Fort knew the ball had to be removed regardless of the risk. Fort's son, George, who was also a doctor, performed the operation, while his father, without anesthetic, gave the necessary directions. The ball finally was extracted and was found to have the teeth marks on it from the enemy soldier who had fired it so long ago during the Twelve Mile Swamp skirmish.

Eddie and his large extended family attended the funeral at the home of Dr. Fort on May 12, 1859. It was a major occasion not just for the family, but for all of Milledgeville. Fort, seventy-two at his death, had been a resident for fifty years and an active and respected citizen. Eddie probably was surprised to see so much attention paid to the elderly man. After all, Eddie had seen Fort only as an old, worn down, somber-faced man.

All the businesses in Milledgeville were closed during the funeral, and all the city officials attended. The state legislature was not in session but many state officials were also present at the funeral. Joseph E. Brown, the governor, led the funeral procession on foot from Fort's home south on dusty Liberty Street and into the City Cemetery (now Memory Hill Cemetery) to the Fort lot.[20] Eddie would have been near the head of the column. The Baldwin Blues, the local militia unit, escorted the casket and fired a volley at the grave. Eulogies were given by the Reverend Mr. Flinn[21] and Dr. Talmage of Oglethorpe University. The *Federal Union* newspaper remarked that "there never has been, within our recollection, so many people present on a like occasion in this city."[22]

The dramatic story of great-uncle Dr. Fort's heroics in this battle may have helped shape young Eddie in this time of increasing war talk prior to the Civil War. Dr. Fort certainly emerged as the legitimate hero at the Battle of Twelve Mile Swamp.

Eddie and his friends, including Tomlinson "Tom" Fort, Jr. and John Fort, sons of Dr. Fort, like most young boys would have played war in the woods and fields. Their enemy may have been imaginary Indians and runaway slaves as in the Twelve Mile Swamp. Perhaps, the enemy at times may also have been . . . Yankees. It also may not be a leap of imagination to believe that two years later, in the spring of 1861, Eddie harkened back to his great-uncle's heroics in a war fifty years earlier, perhaps wishing to distinguish himself in like manner as he entered the military. Could he have imitated the somber face of his great uncle, as he sat for his picture in his Confederate uniform?

Death is hard for anyone to take, let alone a young person.

Sarah likely ached at the thought of another death just a few months after Dr. Fort's death. In late October, Eddie's brother Henry had an accident that resulted in a severe spinal injury. He was put to bed at his grandfather Baradell Stubbs's house and lovingly tended to by his grandmother and aunts.[23] However a spinal injury at that time was generally a death sentence. There was no treatment. All that Eliza and her daughters could do was make Henry as comfortable as possible. All the doctor could do was check in on him from time to time. And all Eddie could do was sit by his dying brother and offer what comfort he could. Henry laid in bed for eleven days, until on the morning of November 4 he finally succumbed to his injuries. Nothing, no friend or family member, could fill the void that was left in young Eddie's life.

It was one more funeral for Eddie to attend. However, this time it was not an honored old man who was being buried with great public outpouring of support. This time it was his own best companion being laid to rest in relative obscurity by his family. It must have been a very depressing day for Eddie. Henry was interred in the Stubbs family lot in the City Cemetery, next to his baby cousin Robert Small Pratt, the infant son of his aunt Julia.[24]

Aunt Julia was pregnant when she attended the funeral. In April she would give birth to a baby boy who would be named Henry Jemison Pratt.

By the fall of 1860, Eddie came home to Louisiana and joined his parents and younger brothers.[25] Sarah may have sensed that Eddie felt a need to be close to his family after Henry's death. And after losing one son, she certainly would have wanted to keep their remaining children closer to home. Eddie had lived in Midway for only three years (1857–1860), but it probably seemed a long time to her.

As the War Between the States approached in 1860, home for Eddie was the plantation in Jackson Parish, Louisiana. Very soon the family moved to the growing town of Monroe, a little over twenty miles from the plantation. Robert, who had been practicing law with his brother-in-law Frank Stubbs,[26] had been appointed as the Register for the Land Office. With his permanent office now in Monroe, it made sense for the family to relocate to the city.

Robert worked alongside George Purvis, an Englishman, who was a fellow attorney and knew Robert from both social and professional circles. George Purvis lived across the Ouachita River in Trenton (present-day West Monroe) with his second wife and six children.[27] His oldest surviving child and namesake was just a few months older than Eddie. Eddie and young George had more than their ages in common; George, too, had lost his older brother when George was nine. Sarah may have imagined that these teenage boys, young men really, formed a friendship through the commonality of loss, and of age. There were not many teenage boys in the town at the time. Monroe had only eighty-nine families in 1860. Trenton was even smaller with just sixteen families. In fact, between the two towns, there were only sixteen teenage boys in 1860, including Eddie, his brother Owen (who was now fourteen), and George Purvis. It was good, Sarah probably thought, that the Jemison and Purvis families socialized, and that Eddie and George were friends.

As Eddie was studying at school with his brothers, and visiting with friends and family, the tide of history was changing. Abraham Lincoln was elected president, and the Southern states began seceding even before he was sworn into office. Shots were fired at Fort Sumter and Louisiana left the Union with other states. Sarah would have remembered the excitement of the time, an excitement tempered with some fear. Perhaps Eddie felt that fear, too. Perhaps that mix of fear with the sadness of leaving home was what was in Eddie's face. But then, she would never know.

Chapter Two

ENLISTMENT TO MARCH 1862

O n April 23, 1861, as mist rose off the Ouachita River, the men who were to become the Pelican Grays were paraded to the courthouse square in Monroe, Louisiana. The grounds of the new courthouse were transformed from a place of law and order to one of excitement and celebration. Flags were flying, fifes and drums were playing, and the cheers of the crowd could be heard by the 114 men who were about to begin their army adventure.[1]

It had been just eleven short days since the first shots at Fort Sumter were fired. The month before Leroy P. Walker, the Confederate secretary of war, requested 1,700 troops from Louisiana. That number was quickly increased to 3,000 when a request for volunteers was made by Louisiana governor Thomas Overton Moore after news of the battle for Fort Sumter was received. Moore's request was followed by yet another one, this time from President Jefferson Davis for 5,000 troops.[2]

In Ouachita Parish, and elsewhere across the state, recruiting officers, some drunk and profane in their zeal to promote the cause of liberty and independence, sought out likely young men to fill the ranks of the new regiments. Eddie's uncle, Frank Stubbs, was one of many men engaged in recruiting as he searched for enlistees for what was to become the company known as the Pelican Grays. Frank may have used newspaper articles, flyers, socials, barroom oratory and other means to drum up patriotism and attract men to fight for Louisiana against the Union.[3] During this time Frank's brother Willie,[4] who had shared the upstairs bedroom with Eddie and who now was secretary and treasurer of the Pelican Grays, started a petition that "cited the strong possibility of war and proposed a full company of infantry volunteers to be organized," in the hopes of raising money to support the men from Ouachita Parish who enlisted.[5] Once the company was formed, its services were offered to the state and the Pelican Grays were ordered to New Orleans.

Eddie was caught up in this military fervor that swept the country. He may have been prompted by the festive and patriotic siren call that brought many of the best and brightest into the ranks of the military. However, his choice may also have been influenced by the memory of his great-uncle Dr. Tomlinson Fort's exploits and fame won at the Battle of Twelve Mile Swamp in 1812.

The men Frank recruited wanted him to be their captain, but Frank declined due to his lack of military experience. Instead, Arthur H. Martin, a twenty-six-year-old lawyer originally from North Carolina, became captain, and Frank took the position of first lieutenant.[6] In total, there were 13 offi-

Monroe, Louisiana, courthouse.
(Kenn Purcell, *A Pictorial History of Monroe, Louisiana*)

Jackson Square, New Orleans, c. 1860. (*Glen C. Cangelosi, M.D.*)

cers and 101 enlisted men. They came from all walks of life: lawyers, doctors, students, merchants, and tradesmen, although most were farmers. Some came from wealth, while others were not wealthy. A few were not even American by birth but chose to take up arms for their adopted home.

Among the enlisted men was sixteen-year-old Eddie, the youngest man in the company. There were several men, both officers and enlisted men, who were not much older than Eddie. In fact, most of the Pelican Grays were in their early to mid-twenties. Living in such a small community, Eddie would have known most of them. Monroe's population in 1860 was only 364 people, not including the slave population.[7] Among the younger men were Eddie's uncle Willie, who was not yet twenty-one. With Frank acting first lieutenant, the send-off that day was certainly a family affair. Doubtless Robert and Sarah came with their three younger sons, Owen, Robert Jr., and Sam. Frank Stubbs's pregnant wife Georgia and their baby daughter would have been there.

The excitement must have been electrifying, for "On that day no one of the company realized but that their departure was anything more than a mere holiday excursion, and that in a few months they would return as victors."[8] Also at the courthouse were eighty men from Jackson Parish who formed the Vienna Rifles, for a total of 192 men departing that day.[9] It was soon time for the men to board the steamboat *J.F. Paragoud* to take them downriver to New Orleans.

The *J.F. Paragoud* was used for shipping cotton up and down the Ouachita River. On this day, though, it was shipping men off to war, and amongst the cheers and "choking sighs,"[10] they marched across South Grand Street from the courthouse to the waiting riverboat that would take them off on their great adventure. For Eddie, it was the adventure of a lifetime.

Two days later, on the morning of the 25th, the *J.F. Paragoud* arrived in New Orleans.[11] The city, at the time the largest in the Confederate States, had been converted from a city of commerce to one preparing for war. A witness, Scotsman William Watson of the Pelican Rifles, wrote:

> All commercial business was suspended. The extensive wharfs along the river which were wont to be crowded with vessels discharging cargo or loading with cotton were deserted. The ships had all cleared out in consequence of the "notice of blockade."
>
> The extensive cotton presses fronting the wharfs were all silent and shut up, and nothing seemed in motion but the preparations for war. The streets resounded with the sound of the fife and drum as different volunteer companies proceeded to the camp of instruction. Carts and waggons [*sic*] moved hither and thither laden with army stores. Newly erected or extended factories were busily manufacturing gun carriages, caissons, and tumbrils, and converting cotton waggons and drags into army waggons.
>
> The constant rattle of steam-driven sewing machines from many buildings announced the extensive manufacture of saddlery equipments, tents, and army clothing, while officers and men in plain uniforms and thoughtful countenances—many of them accompanied by their wives—were seen going in and out of shops purchasing a few articles to take with them which they supposed would conduce to their health and comfort during their life in camp.[12]

Men were pouring in from all over the state. The Lafourche Guards had arrived by railroad the night before.[13] Many companies, such as Walker Guards and Bienville Guards, were from Orleans Parish and were "drilling nightly" with at least twenty more companies on the grounds of Camp Walker in Metairie. They were soon joined by Eddie and the Pelican Grays.[14]

Eddie may have had to wait as long as several days in New Orleans before making the five-mile trek to Metairie. At least one company of men, the Hunter Rifles (4th Louisiana Infantry), was in New Orleans for a number of days before going to Camp Walker.[15] However, the company of the Pelican Rifles was there just a few hours while waiting for their belongings before being marched to camp.[16]

Camp Walker was a bustling place. The camp population was about 1,600 on May 2. A week later it was over 3,000.[17] The Pelican Grays, like the other companies flowing into New Orleans, would have sworn an oath of allegiance to the state of Louisiana, then marched from the wharf to a local hotel to have a hot breakfast and wait to be ordered to Camp Walker.[18]

Camp Walker was located in what in the spring of 1861 was a racetrack.[19] With the racing season ending in early April, and the state needing a location to train its troops, the racetrack was quickly converted into a training camp. "The place was of an oval shape, about a mile and a half in circumference, and enclosed by a close-boarded wall about twelve feet high, with several gates and doors for admission. About forty feet inside of this wall was the course, which was lined on each side by a low but strong wooden paling," wrote William Watson.[20] Robert Patrick of the Hunter Rifles wrote of "spacious brick buildings, comprising of Judges stand, gambling rooms, stables, etc."[21]

Commanded by Brigadier General Elisha Leffingwell Tracy, a Connecticut native who had been living in New Orleans for the past thirty-six years, Camp Walker was far from an ideal training ground.[22] Metairie itself was swampy, "teeming with rank vegetation, through which were deep ditches filled with the drainage from New Orleans, as it moved sluggishly towards Lake Pontchartrain. Within the enclosure the ground had been cleared of the rank grass, but the soil was soft and marshy."[23] The soft soil of the old racetrack quickly turned to mud from the thousands of men drilling and supply wagons churning up the sod. When it rained, the conditions worsened. Eddie may have been one of the men who were forced to sleep outside in the mud, as there were not enough tents and not all without a tent could find shelter in one of the old racetrack buildings. Those lucky enough to procure a tent dug trenches around them to drain the water away from the tent. They slept on hay-stuffed mattresses placed on boards used as flooring so as not to sleep next to the wet ground. Many of the volunteers bought mosquito tents, called "bars," to keep the swarms of mosquitoes at bay while they slept. Those sleeping outside were at the mercy of the mosquitoes at night. Lack of shade left all the volunteers vulnerable to the sun during the day. David Pierson of the Winn Rifles (3rd Louisiana) in letters to his family wrote, "You would not know me on account of my sunburnt face" and "My face is as yellow as pumpkin, so oppressively hot was the sun at Camp Walker."[24]

The temperature in springtime New Orleans averages around 85 degrees. Standing in the hot sun, coupled with high humidity, let alone drilling for hours at a time, would have been brutal. The lack of fresh drinking water would have made conditions even worse for the new recruits. Robert Patrick of the Hunter Rifles wrote that the water was brought in from the Mississippi River "in old pork barrels, and in addition to being warm and muddy, the old grease and salt that had been in the barrels previously gave it a very bad taste."[25]

Food was a little better in that the men did not have to rely on the commissary alone. William Watson wrote, "They had money of their own, and plenty of articles of food and other necessaries were now being exposed for sale in and about the camp and easily obtainable, although anything in the way of cooked food or pastries was not allowed, or at least not encouraged, it being desirable that the men should learn to cook and provide for themselves."[26]

General Tracy's main responsibility at Camp Walker was to turn nonmilitary volunteers into some semblance of soldiers. With only a few days or weeks he could not do much, but at least they could be trained to march together so they could be moved from place to place in columns rather than as a crowd. Although never in the United States Army, Tracy had extensive experience in the state militia, starting with the 4th Militia Regiment, followed by the Washington Artillery, and finally with the 1st Brigade of the 1st Division of the Louisiana Militia with the rank of brigadier general.[27] He saw to it that the volunteers followed strict regulations in their day-to-day activities. Up at 5 a.m., the volunteers had an hour and a half to put up their beds and air their tents, pre-pare and eat breakfast, report in sick if need be, and have their inspection before they began to drill. Drilling would last for three and a half hours, after which the men would break for lunch. This was followed by more drilling and dress parade at 5 p.m. Once the dress parade was finished men had leisure time until lights-out at 9:30. The evenings were "pleasantly spent round the campfires, smoking, talking on different subjects, story-telling, singing, joking card-playing, and other amusements, and occasional visits from friends in other companies until tattoo sounded [at 9 p.m.] when the company was again formed, the roll called, and lights out and off to sleep."[28]

Yet, even with the busy days the volunteers were able, with a pass from a commissioned officer, to venture out of the camp for trips to New Orleans. There they could buy needed items not available in the camp, go out to eat, and in general enjoy the city to the best of their abilities before shipping out.[29] For many this was their first time away from home. That freedom, combined with the excitement in the air at the start of the war, led many young soldiers to make the most of their opportunities for escapades.

It is during his time in New Orleans that Eddie probably had his famous portrait taken. There were many photogra-phers in and near the French Quarter that specialized in por-traits.[30]

Companies had to be placed in regiments before being shipped off to war, and the "most efficient" were incorporat-ed into a regiment first.[31] Just five days after arriving in New

Orleans the 2nd Louisiana Volunteer Regiment was established. As Eddie and the Pelican Grays were part of the 2nd, it did not take long for them to be considered well-trained enough to head to Richmond, Virginia. It was believed that the 2nd would leave either May 1 or 2, but it would be another ten anxious days before the 2nd departed.

The 2nd Louisiana was commanded by Colonel Lewis G. DeRussy, an 1814 West Point graduate. It consisted of ten companies with just over 1,000 men. With the exception of the Atchafalaya Guards, who were from Pointe Couppee Parish (near Baton Rouge), all the companies were from northern Louisiana. Two companies, the Vienna Rifles, who traveled to New Orleans with the Pelican Grays, and the Pelican Rifles, were from Jackson Parish. Eddie may have known men from those companies.

Although the companies were given letter designations by the army, the men referred to themselves by company name.[32] Local newspaper accounts of the various companies in New Orleans also refer to company names and not letter designations. The Pelican Grays took their oath to the Confederacy on May 11 and left for Richmond the following evening by the Jackson (Mississippi) Railroad.[33]

Train travel in the South in 1861 was slow. Most trains traveled at an average of ten to twenty miles per hour due to the low quality of the railroad tracks. Some engines were capable of traveling up to sixty miles an hour, but traveling at the higher speeds was the exception and not the norm. Passenger travel by civilians or the military was far from glamorous. Luxury trains and sleeping cars did not exist and travelers had to make due with "thinly padded and uncomfortable seats."[34] If passenger cars were available, they were used to transport troops. When they were not, troops piled into boxcars and flatcars. Boxcars left the men in stifling conditions longing for air, while flatcars exposed the men to the elements. As the trip consumed several days, Eddie would have traveled, in various degrees of discomfort, on all types

Col. Lewis G. DeRussy

Gen. John Bankhead Magruder. (*Library of Congress*)

of railway cars. The most obvious route would have taken Eddie and the remaining regiments of the 2nd through Mississippi, northern Alabama, Tennessee, and the Appalachian Mountains and on to Richmond. In total, it was approximately 1,200 miles. Between slow speeds, other rail traffic, mechanical difficulties, and stops along the way, the trip probably took about a week.

Sometime prior to June 9 the 2nd Louisiana reached Virginia and settled in on the peninsula between the York River and the James River at Yorktown. The camp at Yorktown held historical significance for the men who pitched their tents on the famous site. For many the new war was a second American revolution, and to find themselves at the place where the British surrendered was important. Perhaps the war could be won right there.

Not much had changed in eighty years. The old earthen fortifications were eroded but still evident. As the men improved and expanded the earthworks, they found bullets, cannonballs, and other artifacts of the old battlefield. Eddie no doubt visited the "Cornwallis Cave" site that still exists.[35]

The overall commander on the peninsula was John Bankhead Magruder, a West Point graduate who hailed from Virginia. When Virginia seceded from the Union, Magruder resigned his commission with the U.S. Army and offered his services to the Confederacy. In April 1861 he was made a colonel in the Provisional Army of Virginia, and three weeks later put in command of the peninsula. Magruder was a character. Known as "Prince John," the fifty-five-year-old officer wrote, sang songs, and enjoyed staging plays and concerts. In particular he liked performing in the leading roles in amateur theater. As it turned out no one could have been better suited for the peculiar requirements the command on the peninsula required.

In the pre-dawn hours of June 10, Eddie, along with the 2nd Louisiana was ordered on a forced march to Bethel Church, approximately fourteen miles south of Yorktown.

The Union army which held Fort Monroe at the tip of the peninsula was advancing up the peninsula through Hampton and Newport News with Yorktown as their goal. If they could break through the Confederate defenses they could, in theory, march right up the peninsula to Richmond. It might just end the war. All available troops were ordered toward Bethel.

Magruder was outnumbered but he had prepared earthworks so he could fight on the defensive. Although they covered fourteen miles in just three hours, Eddie and the 2nd Louisiana reached the battlefield an hour after the battle was over, a march Magruder described as "extraordinary." The battle was a chaotic affair that later in the war would hardly have been noticed. However, so early in the war the two-and-a-half-hour skirmish was important. Only one Confederate was killed and seven wounded. The Union suffered eighteen killed and fifty-eight wounded. Both sides suffered from inexperienced troops and inexperienced officers. During the night march toward the Confederate lines the Union forces had fired into their own columns. With less than 6,000 men on the field only a fraction of them actually saw combat.

Magruder discovered to his dismay that his artillery was not adequate. Gun carriages were so poorly constructed that some broke after a few rounds were fired, making the cannon useless. Cannon ammunition was poor; shells exploded near the muzzle rather than the target. There were also problems with the friction primers, which often failed to ignite the powder charge in the cannons.

Nonetheless, it was a victory, and the South rejoiced far out of proportion to the significance of the event. Magruder became an overnight hero. Newspapers cheered the great success. People who thought that the war would be over quickly looked forward to an end to the hostilities. The entire South was given a huge lift by the propaganda victory. A week after the battle Magruder was promoted to brigadier general. Two months later he was promoted to major general.

As for Eddie, he had a long day. Magruder could not leave

"Federal troops driving the rebels from one of their batteries at Great Bethel," June 10, 1861. This is a torn fragment of a sketch made by war illustrator Alfred R. Waud showing the 5th New York Volunteer Infantry Regiment during the attack near Bethel Church, Virginia, just hours before Eddie Jemison's unit arrived on the scene. (*Library of Congress*)

Yorktown undefended so the 2nd Louisiana had to march back to Yorktown without delay. The exhausted men arrived back at their post by evening after having marched twenty-eight miles and not firing a shot. However, their morale was high; the Yankees had been beaten. The next day they were back to the grind of camp life.

Part of that grind was marching to and fro whenever there was a report that the Union forces were on the move. On June 16 they were back on the line at Bethel. Magruder had about 6,000 men at this time, which was not enough to contain the Union forces, who numbered about 15,000 in and around Fort Monroe. Magruder requested more troops but there were none to send, as commanders in all operational theaters were calling for more. There were just not enough men to fulfill all demands.

On the morning of June 19 Magruder, at Bethel, learned that his pickets had reported that the "enemy was marching in force via Warwick Court House." He wrote his superiors in Richmond, "This, if true would cut us off from Yorktown. I immediately marched for Yorktown, carrying with us such baggage as the wagons which I had (seven in number) permitted, and sent an express to Colonel Hill to order out a regiment at the junction of the York and Warwick roads to stop the enemy, while we took him in rear. He has not yet made his appearance, and we are in the works, but we hear of him in the neighborhood, and I have sent cavalry to feel him. General Butler [Union commander] has called for a re-enforcement of ten thousand men. Please send all you can spare, with plenty of ammunition."

The dash back to Yorktown was not necessary after all. The alleged movement of a large body of enemy troops was a false alarm. Magruder wrote to Richmond the following day explaining the situation and commented that

the embarrassment of operating on the peninsula with a weak force before a strong one is that, if you want to verify a report by a vedette [picket], your force is cut off, and the important point to be defended at all hazards is in danger. This marching and countermarching, however, not being understood, fatigues and dispirits the troops. Still it must be done, as the enemy must be kept in his trenches and fortifications. I had no wagons with me except three loaded with provisions, and had to leave the cooking utensils, some few tents, and the extra rations of our men on the ground.

By now, Eddie knew the road to and from Bethel Church too well.

Once the incident at Bethel Church was over, Eddie and the Pelican Grays settled into camp life at Young's Mill along the Warwick River. It was a mundane life filled with guard duty, eating, drilling, more eating and more drilling, with lights-out at 9 p.m. sharp, only for it to start all over again the next day. Church on Sunday was the only reprieve from the monotony of day-to-day camp life.

Sickness was also a part of camp life, and diseases such as the measles and mumps were running rampant. It is unknown what illness Eddie's uncle Willie had, but he was honorably discharged from service in July, after which he returned home to Milledgeville. Eddie had just lost his first family member.

If Eddie was upset about Willie leaving, there must have been joy at seeing his friend George Purvis arrive at Camp Magruder in August. George had traveled from Monroe to Camp Moore and more than likely requested to be placed with the Pelican Grays. So while Eddie had lost his uncle, he gained his friend.

By October the entire regiment was moved to Camp Pelican, just south of Big Bethel where they settled in for the winter. The fall weather was a bit cooler than what Eddie was used to in northern Louisiana. Daytime temperatures were nice, but sleeping in a tent with temperatures in the forties would not have been comfortable. It is not surprising that

Eddie became sick and was sent to Williamsburg to recover.

Winter quarters should have consisted of wooden houses, but for most of the fall the 2nd still lived in tents. Wood buildings were finally built in the new year, making the mundane life a little more comfortable. Yet there was not much for Eddie to do.

The new year of 1862 also saw the departure of Uncle Frank. Some family or land issues back in Monroe needed his immediate attention, so Frank resigned his post in January and left for Louisiana. Now with both his uncles gone, Eddie was left to lean on his old friend George.

Chapter Three

FIRST BLOOD— THE PENINSULA CAMPAIGN

I n the spring of 1862 the Union goal of capturing Richmond remained. However, the method of doing so had evolved. Rather than going overland as had been tried in 1861, this year's campaign would start at the eastern tip of the peninsula formed by the York and James rivers with a march of eighty-five miles west to the Confederate capital at Richmond. There were many advantages to this plan. The Union army could be protected along its flanks by the navy operating in the James and York rivers. The navy could also hammer the enemy on shore within reach of its heavy guns.

And, the operation did not require storming an enemy beach as Fort Monroe, at the tip of the peninsula, had never left Union hands and would make an ideal safe haven to land the army, its equipment, and its supplies.

The transfer of the Union army to Fort Monroe in the spring of 1862 was a monumental undertaking: 113 steamers, 188 schooners, and 18 barges ferried the army from Alexandria to the peninsula. In one three-week period 121,500 men, 14,592 animals, 1,224 wagons and ambulances, and forty-four artillery batteries plus other equipment made the trip.

The massive military enterprise was led by Major General George B. McClellan, a thirty-five-year-old West Point graduate known as "Little Mac" and the "Young Napoleon." He was a great military organizer and planner well-liked by his men. However, he is best remembered for his obsessive belief that the enemy he faced was always in greatly superior numbers to his own command. This made him a timid commander.

Facing McClellan and his juggernaut for the Confederacy was the flamboyant Major General John Magruder. For the past seven months Magruder along with 5,000 troops, including Eddie and the 2nd Louisiana, were positioned at the south end of the peninsula facing the impregnable Fort Monroe and its 15,000 Yankee defenders. There had been no action other than pickets clashing occasionally. For the soldier it was a dull routine of drills, guard duty, slapping mosquitoes, and attempting to stay warm and dry, as well as working with, and supervising, slaves creating defensive earthworks.

The first line of defense was about fifteen miles up the peninsula from Fort Monroe. Magruder described it as "my real line of defense" and that it "might have been held by 20,000 troops. With 25,000 I do not believe it could have been broken by any force the enemy could have brought against it. Its two flanks were protected by the *Virginia* and

Maj. Gen. George B. McClellan in March 1862 during the Peninsula Campaign. On the left is Lt. Col. A. V. Colburn and on the right is Lt. Col. N. B. Switzer. (*Library of Congress*)

An Army of the Potomac camp at Cumberland Landing along the Pamunkey River, Virginia, in March 1861. According to the photograph, the army's camps covered "thousands and thousands of acres." (*Library of Congress*)

the works on one side and the fortifications at Yorktown and Gloucester Point on the other." Magruder wrote this strong talk on May 3 even though he knew that available to the attacking force were well over 100,000 Union troops plus a massive quantity of artillery, including huge siege guns. However, Magruder was mistaken.[1]

The *"Virginia"* mentioned by Magruder was the C.S.S. *Virginia*, formerly the U.S.S. *Merrimack* that had been scuttled by the Union navy. The Confederates refloated the ship and extensively remodeled it into an ironclad. It was rechristened the *Virginia* although it was more commonly still called the *Merrimack*.

The first indication that something was amiss was a telegram Magruder received on February 27 from his signal officer stationed at Sewell's Point (Norfolk), Virginia, stating that a regiment of infantry had landed at Fort Monroe on the 26th and that six companies of a Massachusetts regiment of light artillery, along with their horses, arrived on the 27th. In addition, 30,000 men would be arriving before March 5. Suddenly, the situation at the end of the peninsula had changed dramatically.

This large-scale movement of Union troops was not unknown to the authorities in Richmond. On February 25 Magruder had been ordered to stand by to reinforce Suffolk, on the south side of the James River, on short notice. Magruder responded on March 1, stating that he could send one regiment and one battery (six artillery pieces) at "great risk here." He took the opportunity to complain that he needed hundreds of slaves to work on fortifying his second line of defense while his "troops were occupying and fortifying the front line where I prefer to fight, but may be forced to leave, as the flanks may be turned by the operations of ships of the enemy." This matter was so urgent to Magruder that he asked that his correspondence of March 1 be forwarded to President Jefferson Davis's secretary of war, Judah P. Benjamin.[2]

On March 3, due to the order to reinforce Suffolk and thus cut his own forces, Magruder withdrew from his first line and took up positions in his second line of defense, which was anchored on his left by the fortifications at Yorktown and by twelve miles along the line of the Warwick River to Mulberry Island, now Fort Eustis, on the James River. Large earthworks were constructed with redoubts, trenches and embankments. The Warwick River runs across the peninsula beginning about a mile or so from Yorktown. Magruder described it as "a sluggish and boggy stream, twenty or thirty yards wide, and running through a dense wood fringed by swamps." There were three dams with the resultant mill ponds behind them. Magruder had his engineers construct three more dams to make the approaches to his defensive line particularly difficult for the enemy. "The effect of these dams is to back up the water along the course of the river, so that for nearly three-fourths of its distance its passage is impracticable for either artillery or infantry. Each of these dams is protected by artillery and extensive earthworks for infantry," wrote Magruder. This line was incomplete and Magruder rushed to complete it using whatever slave labor and soldier labor he could find.

On March 4 Secretary Benjamin wrote addressing Magruder's concerns about the loss of such a large portion of his army:

> We do not believe that you are in the slightest danger of an attack at present, either in front or by being out-flanked by naval forces. All our intelligence tends to one point. Suffolk is the aim of the enemy. Norfolk is to be cut off, if they can accomplish their purpose. If they succeed in this, then, indeed, your entire flank would be thrown open, and you would be forced to fall back rapidly, for they would get possession of all the defenses on the south side of the James River and cross at pleasure at any point they might select. It is for your own defense, as well as that of Norfolk, therefore, that the President desires you

to be ready, at a moment's warning, to re-enforce the army defending Suffolk with at least 5,000 men and two batteries. It is not intended to order you to cross in person or to leave your command, but to send these troops under such general of your command as you may select.[3]

The situation was moving fast. Benjamin wrote Magruder later the same day, "Get 5,000 men and two batteries ready to be thrown across the river as soon as possible. By order of the President." Magruder reacted immediately and ordered Eddie, along with the 2nd Louisiana and three other regiments, be sent to Suffolk. They were to take tents, five days rations, as few cooking utensils as possible, ammunition, spades, and axes.

Fearing he would have to abandon his second line of defensive works, Magruder wrote the adjutant and inspector general in Richmond: "If 5,000 men are taken from this Peninsula and the enemy should advance in force I fear I will be compelled to leave Yorktown to defend itself with a small garrison, the covering work at Mulberry Island with one regiment to defend it, and that with the rest of the troops I shall be forced back to Williamsburg, as there would be three roads to guard with a force of not more than 4,000 men, after deducting the above named garrisons."[4]

To reach Suffolk Eddie and the four regiments marched on March 6 to King's Mill on the James River, where they took a steamer to City Point, near Petersburg. There they took the Norfolk and Petersburg Railroad to Suffolk.[5]

The engagement between the *Monitor* and *Merrimack* on March 9 was not likely to have been witnessed nor heard by Eddie. However, the repercussions of that famous encounter between the ironclads would have a great effect on him.

In the third week of March the Union buildup at Fort Monroe was becoming ominous. In one night twenty transports had arrived delivering troops. Magruder was no longer complaining about not having enough troops; now he was desperately calling for reinforcements. The 35,000 Union troops were now outnumbering him three to one.

The high command in Richmond was in a tight spot. To send troops to Magruder from General Joseph E. Johnston in northern Virginia was dangerous, because those Union troops on the tip of the peninsula could easily be intended as a diversion to draw troops away from Johnston, making him vulnerable to attack. Or the Union troops could be used to move into Norfolk on the other side of the James River. To lose Norfolk would mean that the *Merrimack* would be lost, as the ship's maintenance could only be provided at the base in Norfolk. And, it was only the *Merrimack* that was keeping the James River from becoming a Union highway to Richmond bypassing Magruder and his land defenses.

McClellan arrived at Fort Monroe on April 2. Most, but not all, of his army had preceded him. Not wanting to give the Confederates time to send troops to reinforce the peninsula, he advanced on April 4. This was not a small probing maneuver. Rather, McClellan was planning on marching up the peninsula with a huge advantage in men and artillery to brush aside Magruder's force. He sent columns up both sides of the peninsula. Over 66,000 men and nineteen batteries of artillery were far more formidable than anything he was going to encounter. Deserters from Magruder's army had revealed fairly accurately that other than the troops garrisoning key points along the line of entrenchments, only 8,000 troops were available to cover several miles of the defensive line. This was valuable information for McClellan—yet he did not accept it as truth. His old weakness, overestimating the enemy, clouded his judgment.

On the 5th McClellan's right-hand column encountered the fortifications, along with infantry and artillery, at Yorktown. That was expected. However, the real surprise was when the left-hand column found large earthworks on the far side of the dammed Warwick River. These earthworks created a strong Confederate defensive line from Yorktown to the

James River. Union intelligence somehow had not learned of this line of defense. Even more amazingly the maps did not show the swampy Warwick River stretching across the peninsula almost to Yorktown. Clearly in view to Union observers were thousands of Confederate soldiers. Artillery and musket fire came from the fortified position at Lee's Mill near the James River end of the line.[6] Surprised by the Yorktown-Warwick line of defense, McClellan stopped his advance to reevaluate the situation. Rain that began on the afternoon of April 4 would continue through the 10th, turning the roads into a quagmire and the Confederate trenches into deep pools, hampering McClellan's advance.

The intentions of the Union army were now clear to the Confederacy. The huge army was going to advance up the peninsula. The telegraph flashed the news to Richmond. Richmond notified Johnston to send reinforcements quickly. Magruder would now be sent men as fast as they could be assembled. However, in the meantime he had to hold the line.

Holding was not going to be easy. Magruder had a total of 11,000 men, with 6,000 of them tied down at the fixed garrisons of Mulberry Island, Gloucester Point (on the north side of the York River), and Yorktown. The rest of his line, about twelve miles long, had to be defended by 5,000 men. The information the deserters had given the Union was close to reality: the true odds of 11,000 Confederates vs. 66,000 Union soldiers were dangerously lopsided.

What happened at this critical time was nothing short of incredible. In simple terms Magruder put on a show, a theatrical performance, for the benefit of the Union army. Far more campfires were burning at night than were necessary. Orders were shouted to nonexistent formations. Drum and bugle calls were played for no other purpose than to confuse the enemy. Troops were marched past locations where they would be seen by Union watchers across the lines; then, the men circled out of sight and the same soldiers marched past again, and again. Artillery was fired at any tempting target, then moved to another location and fired again, and again. "Quaker guns," logs painted black and mounted on carriages, appeared to be functional pieces of artillery to Union observers. It was hoped that from the Union lines it would appear as if there were far more men and artillery on the Yorktown-Warwick defense line than were actually there.

It worked. McClellan stopped to await reinforcements before attacking. The delays caused by Magruder's staged illusions allowed the Confederacy the time needed to respond to McClellan's intentions on the peninsula. Mary Chesnut, the famous diarist, wrote, "It is a wonderful thing, how he [Magruder] played his ten thousand before McClellan like fireflies and utterly deluded him—keeping down there ever so long." Magruder would love the allusion to fireflies; it was his finest hour.

It made no sense for Magruder to attempt to defend the line with only a handful of men. Everyone, especially McClellan, knew that. Therefore, McClellan reasoned, Magruder did not have the merely 15,000 men that had been estimated. Magruder must have a large force. McClellan wrote, "Our neighbors are in a very strong position" and "I cannot turn Yorktown without a battle, in which I must use heavy artillery & go through the preliminary operations of a siege." He sent to Fort Monroe for his siege guns and ordered the building of roads to transport the heavy equipment to establish forward supply depots. All of this took time, giving Magruder the time for his reinforcements to come up. The ironic aspect of McClellan's pause to reinforce is that his estimate of 15,000 Confederates was only slightly higher than reality and the only time during the Peninsula Campaign that the estimates were anywhere close to correctly assessing the Confederate strength.

McClellan always suspected that the enemy was in huge numbers. Even when his reinforcements arrived, McClellan determined that the enemy had also reinforced and thus he was still facing very bad odds. As a coward would not arrive at the rank of major general in the United States Army, there must be another explanation for this constant overestimation of the enemy's strength.

One influence on McClellan's judgment was aerial reconnaissance. April 6 brought something new to the battlefield. A tethered hydrogen balloon, the *Intrepid*, rose a thousand feet above the trees, enabling the Union observers to peer deep onto Magruder's stage. Canny "Prince John" allowed them to see only what he wanted them to see: a large army receiving reinforcements making it even more formidable. In fact, reinforcements arrived almost immediately from south of the James River where they had been on assignment. One of those regiments was the 2nd Louisiana with Eddie Jemison.

Thaddeus Lowe, the Union aeronaut, brought several balloons and wagon loads of equipment including two gas generators to the peninsula. His first balloon appeared at Yorktown, the second at the Warwick end of the line. They made daily ascents, sometimes carrying up to four officers equipped with field glasses who would study Confederate troop movements, fortifications, and artillery positions. They could also direct artillery fire. While out of effective rifle range the balloons were targets for enemy artillery, which made observing an adventure. The balloons were equipped with telegraph communications to the ground so McClellan could receive up-to-the-minute information. War had become high tech. Yet, the observers did not detect that they were being fooled by clever John Magruder and his men.

Another influence on McClellan was four Alabama prisoners who told their captors that Magruder commanded 40,000 men and that soon the force would grow to 100,000. Whether these men were planted by Magruder or just took the opportunity to do the Confederacy a good turn will never be known. However, perhaps due to them and perhaps other indicators, McClellan sent Washington a telegram on April

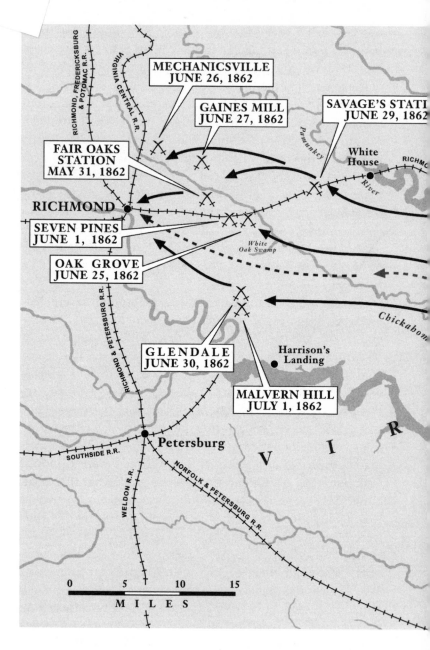

The Peninsula Campaign, June 1861–July 1862.

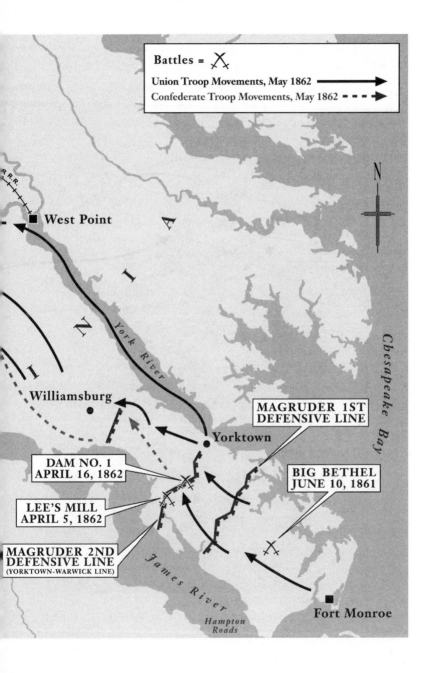

Thaddeus Lowe making observations of Confederate positions in May 1862 from the basket of his balloon, *Intrepid*. (*Library of Congress*)

7, only three days after starting his march, stating that "I shall have the whole force of the enemy on my hands, probably not less than 100,000 men & possibly more." Impressed with Magruder's defensive works, McClellan added, "Were I in possession of their [Confederate] entrenchments and assailed by double my numbers I should have no fears as to the result."[7] These are the words of a man defeated before he has even begun. President Abraham Lincoln responded, writing that delaying an attack would only allow the enemy to become even stronger, and urged McClellan to act.

On April 11 Magruder's command consisted of 34,400 men: two and a half times more men than just a week earlier. He was astonished that McClellan had "permitted day after day to elapse without an assault." Seven days later, after inspecting the defensive works and being unimpressed, General Joe Johnston wrote to General Robert E. Lee, "No one but McClellan could have hesitated to attack."

On April 16, after pondering and examining the defensive line for eleven days, McClellan made an attack at its weakest point, Dam No. 1, in the center of the line. After two days of rain the weather was good, a very welcome change. Eddie Jemison may not have fired his musket much in the past but he got to do so on that Wednesday as the attack was aimed right at the 2nd Louisiana.

The 2nd Louisiana's colonel, William M. Levy, was in overall command during the battle. He wrote that the enemy appeared at 8 a.m. in "considerable force" opposite the position occupied by the 2nd Louisiana Regiment. Two pieces of artillery opened shell fire. It was answered by two pieces of Confederate artillery. This artillery duel continued for six hours while infantry skirmished "at pretty long range." At 3 p.m. six more Union artillery pieces appeared and opened a "furious cannonade, which they kept up with scarcely the slightest intermission, for three hours."

During this cannonade the Confederate earthworks took a heavy pounding. The infantry would have hunkered down behind the earthworks and in trenches for cover. A dry-mouthed Eddie may have thought he was getting used to the sounds of battle, the flying dirt, and exploding shells when at 3:30 enemy infantry rushed across the river, reaching the nearby rifle pits in front of the position occupied by the 15th North Carolina Regiment. The commander of the 15th was killed, resulting in confusion.

Colonel Levy wrote:

> At this time Companies B and D of the 2nd Louisiana Regiment, under the direction of Major Norwood, of that regiment, threw themselves from their position at the redoubt and curtain on the crest of the hill and attacked the enemy along the left of the rifle pits, while the 7th Georgia vigorously attacked them along the rest of the line, and the 8th Georgia came up on the right of the 7th Georgia. Companies I and K, 2nd Louisiana Regiment, stationed at the lower redoubt, near Dam No. 1, opened fire upon the enemy from their position at the redoubt. The rapid and vigorous attack of our troops at once checked the enemy, and in a few minutes they precipitately retreated, re-crossed the creek, and sought shelter, from the havoc which pursued them, under cover of their field pieces. Shortly afterward the movements of the enemy showed that with a large force they intended to renew their effort to break our lines, and with a largely increased force they again attempted to cross, but were speedily repulsed, retreating in disorder.[8]

Company I mentioned in this account was the Pelican Grays of which Eddie was a member. This may have been Eddie's first combat. His colonel commented that in the evening the men "enjoyed the pleasing knowledge that we had repulsed a foe largely exceeding us in numbers." Doubtless, it was a memorable evening for the boys from Louisiana, but they were not able to drink alcohol, as Magruder instituted a no alcohol policy. The general wanted to keep his men under a high level of discipline. He asked

President Davis to declare martial law on the peninsula primarily to more easily control alcohol venders from peddling their wares to the soldiers. Davis agreed.

However "pleasing" the evening may have been, it was also for Eddie a bloody day. Seventy-five Confederates had been killed or wounded. Union dead numbered about thirty-five and another 121 were wounded. As the combat was up close it is very likely that he saw men nearby, men he knew, being torn apart by bullets and shell fragments. With the enemy near at hand it is possible that he also saw men maimed by bullets that he personally fired. Although Eddie may have thought he was seeing war, in fact this was a very minor engagement compared to the horrific carnage that he was to witness first hand in the next eleven weeks.

The battlefield of Dam No. 1, also known as the Battle of Lee's Mill and the Battle of Burnt Chimneys, is located within the Newport News Park where many of the fortifications remain in an excellent state of preservation. Some of the earthworks are twenty feet in height. Dam No. 1 is covered by Lee Hall Reservoir; however, both ends of the dam are visible. There is a footbridge that crosses the reservoir and trails that allow visitors to tour Eddie's battlefield.

The day after the battle at Dam No. 1 Magruder turned over command to the higher ranking General Johnston. Johnston brought reinforcements and there were more on the way. His command included his own plus Magruder's Army of the Peninsula. The combined forces were now called the Army of Northern Virginia.

McClellan settled into a classic siege. On the Confederate side troops and slaves were employed strengthening the earthworks and preparing for the onslaught they knew was coming. Eventually, Southern troop strength would reach about 65,000 and face 113,000 men of the Army of the Potomac. The Union army also entrenched. Roads were built to carry the larger siege guns meant to blow apart the

Confederate defenses. Supply depots were established. What was once thought to be a march to Richmond had bogged down.

Continually, day and night, there were exchanges of artillery as well as musket fire all along the line. The Confederate troops were struggling with boredom, continual noise, occasional casualties, deep mud, not enough shelter, and poor quality food and not enough of it. It rained again on April 20–22. Deep, slippery mud made life miserable. Trenches would fill with water. It was common to stand for hours knee- or even thigh-deep in water while being drenched by rain. Dry clothing was a luxury that was impossible to acquire. Torn and ragged uniforms were standard. Wet, muddy, hungry, and cold was the rule. Sleep was a scarce commodity.

During this period the question of reenlistment arose. Eddie had voluntarily enlisted in May 1861 for one year of service. In fact the great majority of the soldiers had enlisted during the euphoria and excitement of the spring of 1861. The year of enlistment was coming to an end. The Confederacy however could not allow its army to melt away. Incentives such as bounties and furloughs to encourage reenlistment were not successful. The soldiers had seen that war was not as glamorous as they had thought. Something had to be done and done quickly. The solution, passed by the Confederate Congress on April 16, was the Conscription Act, which forced reenlistment upon the one-year volunteers for a term of three years or the duration of the war. In addition, all civilian men between the ages of eighteen and thirty-five would be subject to conscription and forced into the military.

Some soldiers griped that to force them to serve beyond their term was illegal. They had been counting the days until their term expired. Others could see that their views did not carry much weight and they could not do anything about it anyway so were resigned to the situation. A few wanted to reenlist. Also, on the bright side, was the thought that those at home who had not enlisted during the exhilaration after Fort Sumter were now going to be swept into the army by the draft. Throughout the war, and after, men were especially proud if they had been volunteers rather than conscripts.

Of even more interest to Eddie, and his family, was a clause of the Conscription Act: "That all persons under the age of eighteen years or over the age of thirty-five years, who are now enrolled in the military service of the Confederate States, in the regiments, squadrons, battalions, and companies hereafter to be re-organized, shall be required to remain in their respective companies, squadrons, battalions and regiments for ninety days, unless their places can be sooner supplied by other recruits not now in the service."[9] As Eddie would not reach his eighteenth birthday until December he would be discharged from the army on Tuesday July 15, ninety days after the April 16 date set by the Act. In December, he would be eligible for the draft. The tragic nature of this clause as it regards Eddie cannot be overstated.

Eddie's father, Robert, visited in late April. The trip from Monroe, Louisiana, to Virginia made by Robert was an arduous one, covering over 1000 miles. It seems very likely that this journey was prompted by a desire expressed by Eddie to reenlist. Robert would have left Louisiana before the Conscription Act was voted upon. However, the Act did not suddenly appear. It had been talked and argued about for months. Robert would have known, of course, that Eddie had enlisted for one year in May 1861. He would also have known that under the terms of the Act Eddie was eligible for release 90 days after April 16 or before if his *place can be sooner supplied by other recruits not now in the service*. There were no business or personal reasons for Robert to have gone to Virginia other than a son's intention to remain at the front when he could honorably be discharged. Concerned parents would exert themselves, even traveling from Monroe to Virginia, to talk to the young soldier about this extraordinarily important decision. As families back home watched the huge Union army on the peninsula and knew that the outcome of the war might well rest on a climactic battle for Richmond, they shared in the stress felt by the men on the battlefield.

Upon returning home Robert wrote a business letter to a colleague. In that letter, dated June 5, 1862, he included a personal paragraph: "I found Louisiana Troops in Johnston's Army generally in fine health & Spirits. My son particularly so. He was in the fight at Lee's Mill. & seems eager for another. Poor fellows! I fear he may have had quite enough by this time. Reports have just reached us of fighting at Richmond on 29th and 30th. Enemy repulses—our forces in possession of their camps—battle still raging on 31st."[10]

The "fight at Lee's Mill" is now known as Dam No. 1. The reports of fighting on the 29th through 31st were erroneous but serious action was coming. It is impossible to know the literal truth to the statement that Eddie was in fine "spirits" and "eager for another" fight. Was that the bravado of a seventeen-year-old? Surely, Eddie had seen enough combat to know of the potential for frightful wounds and death awaiting on the battlefields. But it is doubtful that he could comprehend the magnitude of the extraordinary violence of a major battle. That would come soon enough. Perhaps he felt invincible or even immortal, as teenagers sometimes feel. He may have also remembered old Dr. Fort and his hero status after the dramatic battle at Twelve Mile Swamp. Although Eddie was the youngest man in his company, he may have felt it was his duty to his comrades to stay and share their fate, that to leave would be letting them down. Or, it may be that young Eddie knew the risks he was facing, considered that the cause he was fighting for was worth the risk, and with full knowledge of the consequences made the brave decision to stay with the army. Whatever the reason, the tone of Robert's letter implies that he was unable to convince Eddie to return home.

Chapter Four

THE DEFENSE
OF RICHMOND

McClellan had decided that a formal classic siege was required to take Yorktown and even wrote his wife requesting that she send him his books on siege warfare. He would dig trenches and put in place over one hundred of his largest siege guns to blast the Confederate fortifications. His men dug zig-zag trenches, working ever closer to the Confederate positions that were getting ready for the bombardment and then the final onslaught of infantry.

On April 29 Johnston wisely reported to Richmond that he could not hold the Yorktown-Warwick line against the massive artillery he faced. "The result is certain," he wrote, "the time only doubtful." Yorktown had to be abandoned. To remain would mean certain defeat and possibly the annihilation of his army. With impeccable timing Johnston began withdrawing his men during the night of May 3. By morning, the works facing McClellan were empty. Another day and Johnston would have faced a devastating attack that could have ended the war since the road to Richmond would have been open to the Union with virtually no Confederate forces to stop the enemy.

The goal was to withdraw the Confederate army and as much of its artillery and equipment as possible to the relative safety of Richmond, sixty miles away. Union cavalry and infantry pursued the retreating army of Joe Johnston. This did not directly affect Eddie as he was on the road several miles to the west, nearer to Richmond. However, the rearguard of the column of retreating Confederates skirmished with the pursuers in the battle of Williamsburg, which allowed the column to get away without being cut off or forced into a major action.

Eddie, along with the 2nd Louisiana, was with Magruder's division marching to Williamsburg, near the head of the column on Lee's Mill Road. He went through Williamsburg, Barhamsville, and New Kent Courthouse to Bottoms Bridge across the Chickahominy River. Here he found the temporary safety of the earthworks around Richmond. Roads were chewed up by the seemingly continual rain and the many thousands of troops, cavalry, wagons, and artillery that had used them on their way east as reinforcements. Progress was very slow and exhausting with mud over shoe-tops and occasionally over calf or even knees. The march was impeded by a long line of wagons and artillery that was in advance of the infantry. The army was bedraggled but had not been beaten militarily. However, the worn-out soldiers knew they had been forced to give up the entire peninsula to the enemy. And that very powerful enemy was on their heels.

The "Magruder" battery at Yorktown following the Federal capture of the Confederate position. (*Library of Congress*)

Abandoned Confederate positions at Yorktown barricaded with cotton bales. (*Library of Congress*)

Magruder was proud of his men. In his May 3 report he wrote,

> From April 4 to May 3 this army served almost without relief in the trenches. Many companies of artillery were never relieved during this long period. It rained almost incessantly; the trenches were filled with water; the weather was exceedingly cold; no fires could be allowed; the artillery and infantry of the enemy played upon our men almost continuously day and night; the army had neither coffee, sugar nor hard bread, but subsisted on flour and salt meat, and that in reduced quantities, and yet no murmurs were heard. Their gallant comrades of the Army of the Potomac [this is a title General Johnston used—he is referring to the Confederate Army of Northern Virginia] and the Department of Norfolk, though not so long a time exposed to these sufferings, shared their hardships and danger with equal firmness and cheerfulness. I have never seen, and do not believe that there ever has existed, an army (the combined armies of the Potomac, Peninsula, and Norfolk) which has shown itself for so long a time so superior to all hardships and dangers. The best drilled regulars the world has ever seen would have mutinied under a continuous service in the trenches for twenty nine days, exposed every moment to musketry and shells, in water to their knees, without fire, sugar, or coffee, without stimulants and with an inadequate supply of uncooked flour and salt meat. I speak of this in honor of these brave men, whose patriotism made them indifferent to suffering, disease, danger, and death. Indeed, the conduct of the officers and men was such as to deserve throughout the highest commendation.[1]

Magruder's report was high praise, but as Eddie plodded through the mud on May 4 he was only thinking of putting one foot in front of the other and being wet, miserable and wondering if food rations would be found somewhere not too far ahead. But meals were not forthcoming. Food depots had not been established to cover a retreat; so he and the others suffered cruelly. When darkness came Eddie slept or tried to sleep along the side of the road in a torrent of rain. The need for speed, the mud, the sounds of nearby skirmishing, and the urgent requirement for no straggling would have been part of Eddie's dismal memories of the retreat.

Defeat was in the air. In Richmond, Confederate government papers were being loaded for shipment to Lynchburg. The Confederate stock of gold bullion was put on a special train for a fast exit should the fall of Richmond become imminent. Civilians were fleeing Richmond with whatever possessions they could fit into a wagon or carriage. President Davis sent his wife and children to North Carolina for safety. In a display of lack of confidence the Confederate Congress not only adjourned but fled the city.

On the anniversary of Eddie's enlistment, May 11, the ironclad *Merrimack*, which had kept the James River free of Yankee gunboats, was blown up to keep it from falling into Union hands. The scenes he witnessed that day, in the mud of the old Williamsburg Stage Road, were a far cry from the jubilation of the prior year. Now, with the James River open to the enemy, no stand could be taken anywhere on the peninsula prior to reaching Richmond; the Union could easily land troops behind whatever line the Confederates made.

The Union ironclads *Monitor*, *Naugatuck*, and *Galena* steamed up the James River heading for Richmond. They were met at Drewry's Bluff by Confederate artillery and a channel blocked with obstructions. The ironclads could not knock out the Confederate batteries nor get past the obstructions and headed back down the river. This was a victory of sorts, just about the only bright spot for the Confederates to savor.

When Johnston's exhausted and hungry army reached Richmond they found newly constructed earthworks. The time they had bought on the Yorktown-Warwick line deceiving the Yankee observers had been used for the construction of defensive lines around Richmond. They took positions within these works as McClellan's forces closed in. It was Yorktown all over again, except this time they could not retreat without losing the Confederate capital. A defeat here might very well end the war. General Johnston offered his resignation but was talked into remaining at his post.

The primary reason the Yorktown-Warwick line was abandoned was because the Union had a large number of heavy siege cannons that once put into place could have devastated the town of Yorktown, as well as the fortifications, troops, and artillery on the line. Now, digging in at Richmond, the troops were to face the same threat. Union forces were so close to Richmond, at places only three miles away, that the forces could, on a quiet night when the wind was right, hear the bells of the city chiming the hours. Something had to be done.

General Johnston must attack McClellan: there really was no other option. The Confederates could not remain behind the earthworks and endure a siege. During the night of May 30 there was a series of thunderstorms of epic proportion. Men on both sides were killed by lightning. Everyone was soaked. The following morning Johnston would strike that portion of the Union army on the south side of the Chickahominy River that ran from north of Richmond to the southeast. The massive Confederate attack would be eastward from Richmond along three roads. The attacks would converge on Fair Oaks station on the Richmond & York River Railroad and nearby Seven Pines. Magruder's corps, of which Eddie and the 2nd Louisiana were a small part, was not involved. They remained in the entrenchments northeast of Richmond guarding the upper Chickahominy bridges.

The battle of Fair Oaks or Seven Pines was confused and ineffectual. The only significant event was that General Johnston was wounded, which required that he be replaced.

President Davis immediately appointed General Robert E. Lee to command the Army of Northern Virginia. The date was June 1.

Lee knew that McClellan could pound him to pieces once his big siege guns were in place. A heavy beating by the siege guns, followed by a final assault with the huge numbers of Union infantry, would finish the job. Lee's only alternatives were to retreat and abandon Richmond or to attack before McClellan could start his bombardment. He needed time to develop a plan to shift McClellan away from Richmond and if all went well to severely defeat him.

Providentially, the skies opened up and rain poured for the first ten days of June making the roads impassable for McClellan's heavy guns. This delay gave Lee time to work. To prevent McClellan from using the still intact Richmond & York River Railroad to bring up his heavy ordnance Lee mounted a long range thirty-two-pound cannon on railroad cars and ran it eastward to keep the Union off the railroad and on the mud roads. This railway gun was unique in that it was armored. The front was covered with railroad track iron at an angle to help deflect incoming projectiles. The rear was covered with bales of cotton to protect the artillerymen. It was known as the Land Merrimack.

Lee set his troops to digging and improving their defenses around Richmond. This was resented by many, who thought digging in the dirt was beneath the dignity of white men. However, better defenses would help keep the Union wolves at bay, which eventually was understood by everyone. The Union soldiers were digging, too, and soon they had impressive earthworks of their own. Dislodging the 100,000 man Union army with the Confederates' 61,000 men seemed impossible. In the night the residents of Richmond could see their army's campfires in the near distance and the glow from the huge enemy's fires farther off and only a few miles away. The situation seemed hopeless.

However, Lee had a plan that, if it worked as designed, would free Richmond from the threat of McClellan and crush the Union forces. The plan involved Lieutenant General Thomas J. "Stonewall" Jackson and his small army in the Shenandoah Valley. When all was ready, Jackson would leave a small force behind in the valley to occupy the Union forces facing him and race to Richmond with 18,000 men, which would help even the odds. The big factor, however, was that Lee would concentrate his strength at only one point on the Union line, allowing the Confederates to overwhelm that portion of McClellan's forces.

The Richmond defenses were to be held by a small force of about 30,000 men facing 75,000 of the enemy. The bulk of Lee's army would shift out of the Richmond defensive line, join with Jackson's men coming from the Shenandoah Valley, and attack the right flank of McClellan's forces on the north side of the Chickahominy River. It would result in 55,000 Confederates attacking 30,000 Union soldiers. In other words, two-thirds of Lee's army would attack one-fourth of McClellan's army on the north side of the Chickahominy. The plan was a risky one. It also meant one-third of Lee's army might have to battle three-fourths of McClellan's on the Richmond defense line.

Jackson would come in on the northeast side of the Chickahominy, the right flank of McClellan. To defend against this flank attack the Union forces would be forced to withdraw from portions of their line facing Richmond along the Chickahominy. As soon as the Union pulled back and left a bridge undefended, the Confederates would march across and continue to roll up the Union right flank.

The Union supply line came from the Union base at White House located on the Pamunkey River, a tributary of the York River. The attack on the Union right flank would threaten that supply line and base. McClellan would have to come out of his Richmond entrenchments to protect his supply line.

While all this maneuvering and resulting combat was taking place, the divisions of Major General Benjamin Huger and Magruder, among them Eddie Jemison, would be manning the earthworks of Richmond. Magruder would be re-creating the show he had performed so effectively on the Yorktown-Warwick line in April. All the old tricks were brought out to create the illusion that the army was far more formidable than it was. Had McClellan realized that a relative handful of men were manning the works he could have attacked Richmond with a force that could not be resisted. Despite Lowe and his observation balloons, the real strength of the defenses of Richmond were never detected by the Union.

Richmond was in great danger when so many defenders ventured out on the offensive. Lee assured President Davis, "If you will hold as long as you can at the entrenchments, and then fall back on the detached works around the city, I will be on the enemy's heels before he gets here." It was a calculated risk that Lee and Davis agreed had to be taken. The operation was a bold move, but to do nothing would result in defeat.

This operation was to start on June 26 with Jackson's arrival. His appearance would force the Union to withdraw from their entrenchments on the right of their line without any action taking place. Unfortunately, Jackson did not arrive. All day Confederate forces waited to go storming across the Chickahominy to aid Jackson but he did not appear. Jackson was unable to get into position in time to meet the intended schedule. Late in the afternoon Major General A.P. Hill ordered his division to cross the river even though Jackson had not yet arrived. The difficulty of timely communication between troop columns at a distance and even knowing where the various columns were created a great deal of confusion: the fog of war.

The result of Hill's attack was the unintended battle of Mechanicsville about four miles north of Eddie in the earthworks on the north side of the Richmond & York River Railroad. The action was out of sight. However, the sound and smoke were plain to Eddie and everyone in Richmond.

McClellan, seemingly eager to see bogeymen behind every tree, was ripe for news of phantom Confederate forces. Allan Pinkerton was chief of intelligence. He relied upon individuals within the Confederate lines to relay information on troop strength and other military matters to him. He would then report to McClellan. Pinkerton's intelligence reports of 180,000 to 200,000 Confederates in the opposing trenches were woefully inaccurate but readily accepted by McClellan. McClellan reported that he had to "contend against vastly superior odds." The troops at Eddie's location helped create that fantasy for McClellan. It was essential for McClellan to believe that the defenses of Richmond were fully manned. Now, with the bulk of the Confederate army engaging in a flank attack, Richmond was very vulnerable. Eddie knew that. He was in the center where an attack was most likely. It was clear to Eddie that the line he was holding was greatly undermanned. Many an anxious look was made across the few hundred yards to the Union earthworks, hoping not to see any sign of attack. It was a very tense period.

During the night of June 26 Eddie and the 2nd Louisiana had shifted their positon a mile to the north from near the railroad to Nine Mile Road just west of the hamlet of Old Tavern. He was still in the entrenchments. The afternoon of the 27th would see the battle of Gaines's Mill about four miles to the northeast of Eddie's position. McClellan's flank was being turned and the battleground was moving to the east. This was a huge battle with 96,000 men involved in furious fighting. Again, however, Eddie could only hear the cannon and musket fire, see the smoke, and imagine what it was like.

The Confederate dead numbered almost 1,500, while the Union lost about 900 killed. This was a tactical defeat for the Union as they left the field to the Confederates. Most impor-

Federal artillery shelling Confederate positions during the battle of Gaines's Mill, Virginia, June 27, 1862. (*Library of Congress*)

tant, this battle convinced McClellan that despite his being within sight of Richmond his campaign was over and he must retreat. His supply base at White House and its supply line to his army was endangered. His plan now was to withdraw his troops to the James River and create a new supply base located there.

Saturday, June 28 became a day of great uncertainty. What was McClellan doing? Where was he going? Lee had to know. If the Union army was retreating down the peninsula, Richmond was safe and pursuit was in order. However, McClellan could have been changing his base of supply to the James River. So it would not do to march down the peninsula, allowing McClellan an opening to make a dash to take Richmond. Or, McClellan might already be moving toward Richmond. Lee struggled with trying to sort through good intelligence, faulty intelligence, partial information, and guesses. He could not afford to be wrong, as Richmond was at stake. By late in the afternoon it was apparent that McClellan was changing his base of supply to the James River and moving his troops in that direction. He had gained a full day on Lee's pursuit.

However, McClellan could not get very far in his one day of grace. Partly this was because the roads did not generally run north-south but rather east-west. Primarily, however, it was because his army was an enormous machine of many parts. The Army of the Potomac had over 99,000 men, 281 pieces of artillery, twenty-six heavy guns of the siege train, almost 4,000 wagons, and 2,500 head of cattle.

The Union army destroyed or attempted to destroy all that they could not carry with them in their retreat to the James River. Railroad engines, along with their cars, were run full speed into the Chickahominy River. Bridges were destroyed. Vast quantities of food was burned or spread out on the ground. The air was filled with the smell of burning bacon.

On the evening of June 28 Eddie was required to remain in the trenches on Nine Mile Road. Since the morning of the 26th he had been on constant alert. While going through their routines of creating the illusion of a large army for Union intelligence to pick up, they had to be ready at a moment's notice to move in cooperation with the main bulk of the army on the other side of the Chickahominy. Or, they might have to repel an attack by greatly superior forces. It was a difficult few days without much sleep and with great anxiety.

Chapter Five

MURDER AT
MALVERN HILL

On the morning of Sunday, June 29, Eddie received orders to move out of the trenches he had been occupying on Nine Mile Road. The 2nd Louisiana was joining in the attacks on McClellan and the massive operation to force the enemy away from Richmond. They had slept, if they slept at all, in the trenches because they might have been called at any time to advance or repel an attack. Early morning reconnaissance revealed the enemy had pulled out of their fortifications during the night. The enemy withdrawal was a momentous time for the

Confederate troops. They had been hearing the sounds of battle in the near distance since the 25th when the Seven Days battles began. Powder smoke had been visible, and many wounded and refugees from the fighting had been making their way to Richmond. For Eddie the tension of waiting for a potentially overwhelming attack was over. Now he was moving east through the unoccupied Union earthworks and beyond. A new tension replaced the old. He was going out to meet the enemy. And he knew this was not going to be a skirmish like that at Dam No. 1 two months earlier.

Orders were to take the Williamsburg Road and the tracks of the Richmond & York River Railroad toward the east. It had been hot and dry the last few days, which improved the roads significantly. Eddie noticed that the countryside he passed through was much different from what it had been in May when he had retreated to Richmond after defending the Yorktown-Warwick line. Since then the Union army had been here. Vast numbers of trees and fences were gone to make campfires. Fields and roads were dug up and rutted by innumerable wagons and artillery plus many thousands of marching feet. Debris was everywhere, as was the look of desolation and destruction. Some areas had seen fighting with its resultant rubble and stench.

The sound of artillery and musket fire came from various directions, although there was nothing truly alarming in the immediate vicinity. As they approached Savage's Station it was reported that the enemy was ahead. The 2nd Louisiana, part of the brigade of General Howell Cobb,[1] formed in line of battle on the left of the line. In line of battle the several regiments continued the march to Savage's Station without encountering the enemy. Upon reaching Savage's Station they were fired on by the enemy and replied with artillery that drove the enemy off.

Late in the afternoon and evening the battle of Savage's Station was fought. Eddie was present; however, he was positioned on the left side of the railroad and Cobb's brigade was not actively engaged. Eddie did get a front-row seat to the battle taking place one half mile to their right. This was another fouled-up battle. Among other miscues Stonewall Jackson was supposed to arrive but never did: he sent a message saying he had "other important duties to perform" which never were explained. In any case, Eddie witnessed the battle but did not take part. The battle ended at 9 p.m. with a thunderstorm drenching the participants. The Union losses were about 900, twice the casualties of the Confederates. Despite a steady rain Eddie tried to get some sleep on the battlefield that night.

Eddie also witnessed the railway gun, the Land Merrimack, in use. This ingenious combination of railroad cars, a locomotive, and a heavy gun had limited usefulness as the gun could not be turned much and basically had to fire in line with the railroad tracks. Also, it was vulnerable if the track behind was damaged by enemy fire because it could not then be withdrawn. At Savage's Station the Land Merrimack attracted a lot of enemy fire. It was backed down the track to safety.

The battlefield of Savage's Station is today entirely consumed by the intersection of Interstates I-64 and I-295 east of Richmond. Eddie's position with Cobb's brigade would be in the northwest quadrant of the intersection, just beyond the cloverleaf. He would have stood in line of battle just to the east of present day Dry Bridge Road and south of Meadow Road.

Infantry was the backbone of Civil War military. Huge lines of men would stand shoulder to shoulder to fire . . . and to receive the enemy's fire. Despite the four-hundred-yard effective range of the Civil War musket, the linear tactics were much the same as those of the American Revolution or the Napoleonic Wars. The practical characteristic of lines of men was that they were the only way the troops could be moved under fire. These lines of men carried tremendous firepower when their fire was concentrated. A trained soldier could load, aim, and fire his muzzle-loaded weapon three times per minute. That may not sound impressive; however, when a thousand-man regiment fired three thousand rounds in one minute, a great many casualties could be expected. And when necessary, the infantryman could follow up his firing with the bayonet.

On the road, regiments usually moved in columns of four. On the battlefield it was difficult for the officers to communicate orders to their men. Shouting through the noise of artillery and musket fire would only reach the nearest men. Therefore, it was necessary for soldiers to keep in close contact, elbows touching, so men would be guided by the movements of those around them. With much practice this unsophisticated communication system worked. Men were also trained to keep an eye on the flag. Where it moved the soldiers would follow.

As Eddie's brigade commander, General Cobb had duties that included going into battle with his men and controlling their actions. In the case of Malvern Hill, Cobb led three regiments into battle, the 24th Georgia, the 15th North Carolina, and the 2nd Louisiana. In line of battle each regiment would be in two long ranks with the regiments lined up next to each other. It was Cobb's responsibility to make sure that the regiments had a clear field of fire, and did not overlap or fire into a friendly unit. Cobb could also order changes in direction. Regimental officers assisted the brigade commander by getting their men to follow the orders.

When going into battle the men would be ordered to change to line of battle formation. Eddie was trained to go forward, backward, and at angles on command in line of battle. They could also break and re-form to get past obstructions.

Often the term "charge" is used to describe a rapid advance. This was not a case where lines of men ran toward the enemy. To keep control it was necessary that the line of battle be maintained. If the men ran at will the faster men

Gen. Howell Cobb. (*Library of Congress*)

A makeshift Federal field hospital at Savage Station, Virginia. Among the wounded are those who fought at the battle of Gaines's Mill on June 27. The hospital was captured when the Confederates overtook the area two days later. (*Library of Congress*)

would outpace the slower and it soon would simply be a mob out of control. At a pace of 110 steps per minute, the line would advance about 85 yards per minute. This pace could be maintained for extended periods of time. However, under heavy fire the order may be given to increase the pace to double-quick time, which would be 165 steps per minute, allowing the regiment to cover 150 yards per minute. Frequently an attack would be halted to realign the lines, as it was important that they be maintained in good order to maintain firing effectiveness or direction of advance.

Communication on the battlefield was extremely complicated and always difficult. Huge groups of men, in many locations, out of sight of each other, ideally should act in coordination. In theory, there is someone in overall command who knows what is going on everywhere on the battlefield. This commander would also know where each unit was positioned. Orders would be given, received promptly, thoroughly understood by the recipient, and accurately carried out. For many reasons this simply would not often happen. Sometimes even large units found themselves going down the wrong road miles from the battlefield and did not know they were mistaken, and no one in overall command knew where they had gone. Occasionally, a brigade commander, for example, would not know where all of his regiments were physically located. Orders were frequently delayed in getting to the recipient; sometimes orders were delivered hours late. Some orders were never delivered. Sometimes the orders were written in vague or unclear language, leaving the recipient either wondering what the order meant exactly or confidently following the orders but taking the wrong action because the order had been misinterpreted. Orders sometimes did not have times written on them so the recipient could not know if one order superseded another.

To make things even more difficult, the overall commander may not have had the information he required to make sound decisions and issue sound orders. Timely information as to what the enemy or friendly forces were doing, where friendly and enemy forces were located and the nature of the terrain all across the battlefield may have been unavailable, incomplete, or entirely erroneous. Additionally, the extreme fatigue of the senders and recipients of these messages must be considered. For the week prior to Malvern Hill few had had much sleep; this included the officers commanding. All of these elements of the "fog of war" are possible in any battle, and virtually no battle has no fog. However, the battle at Malvern Hill had far more than its share of fog.

On Monday morning, June 30, Eddie awoke to find that the enemy had again slipped away in the night. Left behind was their hospital with 3,000 sick and wounded. Supplies of all sorts had been burned or poured out on the ground. Destruction, debris, and the casualties of the battle were widespread.

Lee's plan for the day was the same as before: attack McClellan on his march and bring him to battle. McClellan's army was strung out for miles on their way to the James River. Lee wanted to converge on the little village of Glendale and cut the retreating columns in two and perhaps literally win the war with a massive victory. Lee would strike with 71,000 men against 61,500. Magruder's division, including the 2nd Louisiana, had a minor role acting as a reserve and never came to action.

Monday, June 30, 1862, was one of the hottest of days. To make it worse Eddie marched for eighteen hours and covered over twenty miles that Howell Cobb described as "most fatiguing." At least the roads were not muddy. Instead, he endured clouds of fine dust, arriving at the scene of the Battle of Glendale at 3 a.m. on Tuesday, July 1. Cobb's brigade relieved Lt. Gen. James Longstreet's men who had fought in the battle. The battle at Glendale, also known as Frazier's or Frayser's farm, had been bloody. The Union lost about 300 killed and 1,700 wounded. The Confederates lost over 600 killed and over 2,800 wounded. The battlefield would be a

horrific place for Eddie to bed down for the night, surround-
ed by the endless cries of the wounded, the shadowy figures
going over the field helping the wounded, searching for comrades, burying the dead, and the wounded trying to walk or
crawl away.

Colonel John B. Gordon slept on such a field a few nights
before. He "dropped down on the ground for a much-needed
rest. In a few moments I was sound asleep. A slightly elevated
mound of earth served for a pillow. Frequently during the
night I attempted to brush away from my head what I
thought in my slumber was a twig or limb of the underbrush
in which I was lying. My horror can be imagined when I discovered, the next morning, that it was the hand of a dead soldier sticking out above the shallow grave which had been my
pillow and in which he had been only partly covered."[2]

The Battle of Glendale was inconclusive. However, from
the Southern point of view it was a failure. The lack of coordination of the units involved allowed the Union army to
escape rather than be cut in two and defeated. All day
Monday, June 30 and throughout the night McClellan's army
crept down congested roads to Malvern Hill and the safety of
the gunboats on the James River. The morning of Tuesday,
July 1 revealed once again that the enemy had slipped away
during the night.

This was the last chance Lee had to cripple McClellan's
army before it reached the safety of the James River.
However, unlike the past few days, Lee would not be attacking the retreating Federal column but rather attacking a position three miles away at Malvern Hill prepared by the Union
the night before.

The battlefield at Malvern Hill is at the intersection of
two principal roads that merge for a time. Willis Church
Road runs from the northeast to southwest. Carter's Mill
Road runs from Long Bridge Road in the northwest to the
southeast. Carter's Mill Road and Willis Church Road merge
at the Malvern Hill battlefield for a distance of about four-

tenths of a mile where they run directly north-south before splitting to go their separate ways. The main action of the battle was in the vicinity of this junction.

Eddie and the 2nd Louisiana as part of Howell Cobb's brigade were located to the west of Carter's Mill Road. Their attack was focused on a section of the Union line located halfway down and on the west side of the merged section of Carter's Mill Road and Willis Church Road. The following discussion focuses on that area, the Confederate right, as this is the area Eddie could see and where he fought.

Stonewall Jackson was ordered to march south on Willis Church Road, which he did. Magruder was to take his forces, which included Eddie and the 2nd Louisiana in Cobb's brigade, southwest along Long Bridge and Road then turn south on Carter's Mill Road. However, through miscommunication and poor maps Magruder went several miles too far on Long Bridge Road. Magruder, following the advice of his local guides, then turned left on another road heading south. Eventually, they were turned around and marched back on Long Bridge Road then turned right, south, onto Carter's Mill Road. After marching and counter marching several hours in the dust and sun Eddie reached the battlefield after 4 p.m.

The Carter farmhouse, just to the left (east) of Eddie's position, was located about 1,600 yards, or nine-tenths of a mile, north-northwest from the line of Union artillery and infantry on Malvern Hill—the goal of their attack. The Carter farmhouse was within range of the Union artillery and under fire.

Malvern Hill is not what many would consider a "hill" at all as seen from the north, the Confederate view. Eddie saw a gently sloping open plateau of farmland. The hill was a superb place to defend. Douglas Southall Freeman wrote, "Had the Union engineers searched the whole countryside below Richmond, they could not have found ground more ideally set for the slaughter of an attacking army."[3] The

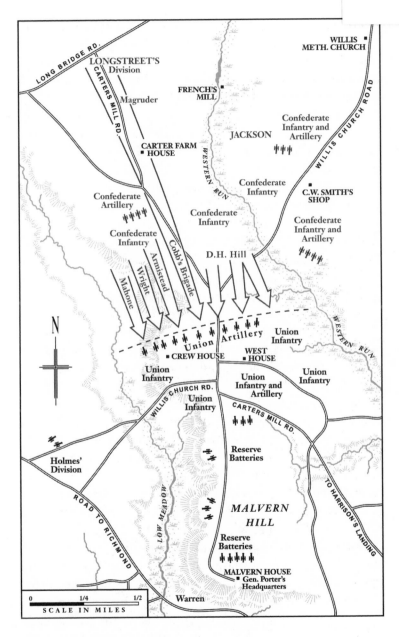

The battle of Malvern Hill, July 1, 1862.

Union view looking north to the west of Carter's Mill Road, from where Eddie would attack, revealed farmland rolling downward then rising again at Carter's farm. The vast majority of the field of fire was unobstructed with only a few very minor undulations where men might find hope of cover.

At the morning meeting with Lee, Magruder, and Longstreet, General D. H. (Harvey) Hill[4] commented that one of his chaplains who was from the Malvern Hill area had given Hill a description of the terrain. It was excellent for defense. Hill said, "If General McClellan is there in strength, we had better let him alone." Longstreet laughed, "Don't get scared, now that we have got him whipped." Lee did not reply.[5] Many of the commanders, including Lee, believed that the Union army was demoralized, as the Confederates had picked up many stragglers and the roads were choked with abandoned equipment and burned supplies in the wake of the retreating army.

Artillery was placed along the Union line on the top of the gentle slope of Malvern Hill. The cannons were spaced far enough apart that they could be easily turned toward any desired target. There were thousands of infantry behind the artillery. To the rear of the infantry were larger guns and even heavy siege guns. In the James River a mile or so to the rear were gunboats that could lob shells onto the battlefield.

The Confederate strategy was to bring up their own artillery, over one hundred pieces, and hit the Union artillery hard enough that attacking infantry could then sweep the hill. A site for the artillery was selected on the Confederate right on a knoll south of the Carter farm and another on the left. Unfortunately, the Confederates could not bring up their guns in a timely fashion. Later, General D. H. Hill described their performance as "farcical." Longstreet wrote that "the enemy concentrated the fire of fifty or sixty guns upon our isolated batteries, and tore them into fragments in a few minutes after they opened, piling horses upon each other and guns upon horses." On the knoll on the right the

Confederate artillerymen would fire their guns then run the guns back down the far side of the knoll seeking shelter from incoming Union fire. They reloaded then brought the guns back into position. The reprieve was only temporary, as the Union fire against the Confederate artillery was devastating. One Union six-gun battery fired over 1,300 rounds during the afternoon. The entire battlefield at Malvern Hill could be, and was, effectively within sight and range of the Union artillery.

At Malvern Hill the field artillery fired a variety of projectiles depending on the target and the distance to the target. Solid shot was used against buildings and massed troops. From a smoothbore it was effective out to 1,700 yards. Shells, which were hollow projectiles containing explosives which would break the projectile into fragments, were set off using a time fuse. They were primarily used in attacks on troops behind earthworks, under cover, or in woods with an effective range of 1,300 yards. Spherical case was much like a shell, except instead of the projectile itself simply breaking apart into pieces, the spherical case contained musket balls. It was very effective against troops up to 1,500 yards. Up close, under 400 yards, the antipersonnel round of choice would be canister, which was a metal can containing iron balls. The can would rupture on firing, sending out the iron balls much like a huge shotgun.

The Yankee gunboats in the James River also provided some heavy artillery fire. However, as the gunners could not see where their shot landed they had to be directed by semaphore and compass bearings. Their fire was not accurate, but their large shells had a psychological impact on the Confederates. The gunboats hit several Union positions and they were ordered to cease firing.

Brigadier General Lewis Armistead's brigade, positioned just west of Carter's Mill Road, noticed Yankee skirmishers approaching close enough that the Confederate artillery was within their range. Armistead moved three regiments forward to drive them back, which was done successfully. However, Armistead's men received tremendous musket and artillery fire from Malvern Hill. Rather than returning through the dangerous incoming fire, they advanced to a small ravine that was actually nearer to the Yankee line on Malvern Hill. There, pinned down, they clung to the ground as enemy fire passed closely over their heads.

Shortly after, about 4 p.m., Magruder arrived on the field. His troops, of which Eddie was a part, had yet to arrive. Magruder sent a captain to notify Lee that he was present on the battlefield. The captain was also to report to Lee that three regiments of Armistead's had succeeded in getting part way up Malvern Hill. This captain reported to Lee at the same time that Lee received a report that Union troops had been seen withdrawing from Malvern Hill. Actually, those troops were not withdrawing but taking cover from the incoming artillery fire. However, at that moment it appeared to Lee that McClellan was once again retreating and Armistead's regiments were advancing.

Lee gave Magruder's captain orders to take to Magruder. This captain wrote down Lee's orders: "General Lee expects you to advance rapidly. He says it is reported the enemy is getting off. Press forward your whole line and follow up Armistead's success." The wheels were set in motion and could not be stopped. After the battle Lee sought out Magruder and asked him why he had attacked such a formidable position. Clearly, Lee had not meant the order given to the captain to be carried out without using judgment; but Magruder understood the order as one with no discretion. Magruder replied to Lee that he had been ordered twice to attack. And he was right.

In fact, when Lee's orders, relayed by the captain, arrived, Magruder had just received an order written hours earlier by Lee's chief of staff which had been sent to the division commanders: "Batteries have been established to act upon the enemy's line. If it is broken as is probable, Armistead, who can witness effect of the fire, has been ordered to charge with a yell. Do the same." This order had no time written on it. Magruder assumed it was current. Magruder now believed he had two orders from Lee commanding him to attack.

Communication across a battlefield by the "yell" or shout of a brigade was neither effective nor practical. The yell could have been from any cause, from any body of men, including Union forces. The opportunity for error was enormous. A courier on horseback, perhaps with a backup courier due to the possibility of one messenger being killed, would have been far more reliable. Also, the fact that a major battle could be initiated by a sole brigadier general's limited view of the battlefield reveals the uncertainties of commanders' decision making in the chaos of combat.

At 5:30 p.m. Magruder opened the battle by sending forward the brigades of Brig. Gen. William Mahone and Brig. Gen. Ambrose R. Wright.[6] When Mahone and Wright left the woods and entered onto the open ground they let loose with a Rebel yell. Wright's brigade got ahead of Mahone. They were met with Union artillery and musket fire. One survivor wrote, "It is astonishing that every man did not fall; bullet after bullet, too rapid in succession to be counted . . . shell after shell, illuminating the whole atmosphere, burst over our heads, under our feet, and in our faces."[7] Wright's men, at least those who survived, ended up in a slight depression three hundred yards from the Union line and could not go forward or back. Mahone's brigade made its charge and was driven back.

It will be recalled that the early order from Lee was to attack when a yell was heard from Armistead's brigade, which would indicate that Armistead had seen that the Confederate artillery barrage had been effective in destroying the Union position. Armistead's men never yelled because the Confederate artillery had not been effective. However,

Mahone's and Wright's brigades did yell. Hearing their yell, D. H. Hill mistakenly thought it was the signal yell from Armistead, and he ordered his five brigades to attack. That was just the beginning.

Brigade after brigade was fed into the jaws of the enemy artillery and infantry. There was little or no coordination to the attacks. The conveyor belt of men was simply feeding them forward to the same end.

Colonel Gordon accompanied the 3rd Alabama Regiment in its attack. He describes his ordeal:

> I made the advance, but the supports did not come. Indeed, with the exception of one other brigade, which was knocked to pieces in a few minutes, no troops came in view. Isolated from the rest of the army and alone, my brigade moved across this shell-ploughed plain toward the heights, which were perhaps more than half a mile away. Within fifteen or twenty minutes the centre regiment with which I moved, had left more than half of its number dead and wounded along its track, and the other regiments had suffered almost as severely. One shell had killed six or seven men in my immediate presence. My pistol, on one side, had the handle torn off; my canteen, on the other, was pierced, emptying its contents—water merely—on my trousers; and my coat was ruined by having a portion of the front torn away: but, with the exception of this damage, I was still unhurt. At the foot of the last steep ascent, near the batteries, I found that McClellan's guns were firing over us, and as any further advance by this supported brigade would have been not only futile but foolhardy, I halted my men and ordered them to lie down and fire upon McClellan's standing lines of infantry. I stood upon slightly elevated ground in order to watch for the re-enforcements or for any advance from the heights upon my command. In vain I looked behind us for the promised support. Anxiously I looked forward, fearing an assault upon my exposed position. No re-enforcements came until it was too late. As a retreat in daylight prom-

ised to be almost or quite as deadly as had been the charge, my desire for the relief which nothing but darkness could now bring can well be imagined. In this state of extreme anxiety a darkness which was unexpected and terrible came to me alone. A great shell fell, buried itself in the ground and exploded near where I stood. It heaved the dirt over me, filling my face and ears and eyes with sand. I was literally blinded. Not an inch before my face could I see; but I could think, and thoughts never ran more swiftly through a perplexed mortal brain. Blind! Blind in battle! Was this to be permanent? Suppose re-enforcements now came, what was I to do? Suppose there should be an assault upon my command from the front? Such were the unspoken but agonizing questions which throbbed in my brain with terrible swiftness and intensity. The blindness, however, was of short duration. The delicate and perfect machinery of the eye soon did its work. At last came, also, the darkness for which I longed, and under its thick veil this splendid brigade was safely withdrawn.[8]

We left Eddie and the 2nd Louisiana along with the 24th Georgia and 15th North Carolina just west of the Carter house, north on Carter's Mill Road with Brigadier General Howell Cobb. There, Cobb received a message from Armistead, who was pinned down, requesting support. Cobb immediately put his brigade into motion. Eddie would have seen the grim sight of the still smoking Confederate artillery position west of Carter's Mill Road as he passed through it. Wounded and dead horses and dead men along with dismounted artillery pieces were strewn around the chewed up earth where incoming artillery rounds had thoroughly destroyed the battery. This position was 875 yards from the Union line.

Far off on the Confederate right and beyond the sight and knowledge of Eddie, the 1st Georgia regiment attacked Malvern Hill. Eddie's boyhood friend, and second cousin, Tom Fort (Lt. Tomlinson Fort, Jr.), was struck in the chest by a shell fragment. Severely wounded, he was left on the field for dead. However, he lived to be wounded again at the battle of Second Manassas.[9]

A general with binoculars was not needed to see the enemy. The Federal artillery was clearly visible to Eddie as he advanced with a dry mouth and rapid heartbeat. The ground behind the artillery was black with thousands of Union infantrymen. It also did not take a general to understand that this advance was extraordinarily dangerous. Eddie, even with little experience, saw that he was in a horrific situation. He was crossing a broad plain, roughly a half mile, in full view of the enemy armed with many well-manned cannon that were constantly firing. The ground before him was not clear, as it had been a few hours earlier. It was now littered with dead or wounded men and horses. The air was filled with white smoke and bullets zipping past. The ground shook from exploding shells. The deafening noise was continuous. All human senses were overloaded. This was madness.

Howell Cobb wrote,

> We had to pass through the open field in our front under the fire of the enemy, which was done in double-quick and good order, and had to pass through dense woods and almost impassible ravines, which separated us from General Armistead's position, all of which was done in quick-time and with alacrity by the three regiments. On reaching this point I immediately posted my command on the crest of the hill in front of batteries of the enemy, which continued to pour a deadly fire upon that point, as well as the entire distance which we had traversed from the ravine near Mrs. Carter's house. Our duty was to prevent any advance of the enemy and to unite at the proper time in the effort to carry the batteries of the enemy. We had not occupied this position long when General Magruder was informed that the enemy was advancing in our front, and under his order I at once advanced these three regiments to the open field in front

of the batteries of the enemy. The advance of the enemy was repulsed and the regiments united in the general assault on the batteries.

The conduct of both officers and men throughout was all that could be asked and even more than could be expected of men. The best evidence I can offer of the daring and courage of the men of my command is the fact that after the battle their dead were found mingled with those of other brigades nearest the batteries of the enemy.

It was at this point in the battle that Colonel Norwood, of the Second Louisiana, while gallantly leading his regiment, fell severely, but, I am happy to say, not mortally, wounded [Norwood actually died of his wounds]. Major Ashton, of the same regiment, had seized the colors of the regiment after three brave men had been shot down in the act of bearing them forward, and was bravely cheering on his men and rallying them to their standard, when, pierced by several balls, he fell and died instantly.

. . . It is but justice to the men of my command to state the fact that for more than forty-eight hours previous to the battle they had had neither rest nor food; and though their ranks had been greatly reduced by exhaustion, there was no murmuring or spirit of complaint as long as there was an enemy in front.

We commenced the march from the burnt chimney on the morning of June 29 with 2,700 men, but fatigue and exhaustion had so reduced our ranks that less than 1,500 were carried into the battle of the 1st instant, and of that number nearly 500 are in the list of killed and wounded.[10]

After it was over one survivor wrote:

At first sight it seemed that the enemy was massed between their cannon in double column closed in mass. The enemy opened the most terrific and destructive fire in the face . . . that ever any troop met since the world began. Within five minutes it was impossible to distinguish one man from another on account of the smoke and the dust caused from the cannon in our immediate front. The men would rush forward as they were urged, and then it seemed as though the whole line would sway back as a field of corn would before a wind. Though the sun was shining bright, when we went in everything was soon so dark one could scarcely see. Men were falling like leaves in an autumn wind.[11]

General D. H. Hill believed that over half of the Confederate casualties were caused by artillery, which was extraordinary in that era. It was more usual for artillery to account for 10 percent of the casualties. He participated in the attack and wrote:

> I never saw anything more grandly heroic than the advance after sunset of the nine brigades under Magruder's orders. Unfortunately, they did not move together, and were beaten in detail. As each brigade emerged from the woods, from fifty to one hundred guns opened upon it, tearing great gaps in its ranks; but the heroes reeled on and were shot down by the reserves at the guns, which a few squads reached. Most of them had an open field half a mile wide to cross, and this under the terrible fire of field artillery in front, and the fire of heavy ordnance of the gun-boats in their rear. It was not war—it was murder.[12]

Union general Fitz John Porter viewed the carnage from the Union vantage point:

> The artillery . . . mowed them down with shrapnel, grape, and canister; while our infantry, withholding their fire until the enemy were within short range, scattered the remnants of their columns, sometimes following them up and capturing prisoners and colors. As column after column advanced, only to meet the same disastrous repulse, the sight became one of the most interesting imaginable. The fearful havoc of the rapidly bursting shells from guns arranged so as to sweep any position far and near, and in

Federal artillery firing into the Confederate lines at Malvern
Hill. (*Library of Congress*)

THE BATTLE OF MALVERN HILL, Vᴬ JULY 1ˢᵗ 1862.

A Currier & Ives lithograph of the battle of Malvern Hill showing the 36th New York Volunteers capturing the colors of the
14th Regiment of North Carolina. (*Library of Congress*)

any direction, was terrible to behold. The terrific hail could not be borne, and such as were left of the diminished columns precipitately fled or marched rapidly to the rear, sometimes followed by our infantry, whose shots leveled many more of their brave men.[13]

It was into this maelstrom of death that Eddie charged side by side with his friend George Purvis and disappeared. Casualties were high. The 2nd Louisiana lost 182 killed and wounded, more than all but one other Confederate regiment. It is unknown how many men of the 2nd Louisiana went into the battle, as many had dropped out in the previous days of marching, but the percentage of casualties clearly is appalling.[14] It was said later that Eddie and George were killed by the same shell.[15] They died alongside other young men who had boarded the steamship *Paragoud* just fifteen months earlier for their adventure of a lifetime.

Battle raged through the evening until darkness finally put an end to the carnage.[16] When it was fully dark, men from both armies wandered across the field carrying lanterns as they attempted to care for their comrades. Informal truces were agreed upon by some of these small groups. Yet occasionally there were flashes of gunfire in the darkness. A few roamed the battlefield stealing from the dead. It was a scene from a nightmare.

Union cavalry colonel William W. Averell wrote long after the war about the early morning of July 2, the day after the battle. He was commanding the rear guard and positioned at the former line of the Union artillery. The Union army had withdrawn during the night.

By this time the level rays of the morning sun from our right were just penetrating the fog, and slowly lifting its clinging shreds and yellow masses. Our ears had been filled with agonizing cries from thousands before the fog was lifted, but now our eyes saw an appalling spectacle upon the slopes down to the woodlands half a mile away.

Over five thousand dead and wounded men were on the ground, in every attitude of distress. A third of them were dead or dying, but enough were alive and moving to give to the field a singular crawling effect. The different stages of the ebbing tide are often marked by the lines of flotsam and jetsam left along the sea-shore. So here could be seen three distinct lines of dead and wounded marking the last front of three Confederate charges of the night before. Groups of men, some mounted, were groping about the field.

As soon as the woodland beyond, which masked the enemy, could be clearly seen, I offered battle by directing the infantry lines to show on the crest, the sham sections of artillery to execute the movements of going "into battery, action front," and the flank squadrons to move toward the enemy until fired upon. All these details were executed simultaneously at the sound of the trumpet. The squadrons had not proceeded three hundred yards when they were fired upon and halted. At the same time, a horseman from among those on the field approached our line with a white flag. An aide was sent to meet and halt him. The Confederate horseman, who was an officer, requested a truce of two hours in which to succor their wounded. I was about to send a demand that his request be put in writing, when I reflected that it would be embarrassing for me to reply in writing, so word was sent to him to dismount and wait until his request had been submitted to the commanding general. In the meantime the scattered parties of the enemy withdrew hastily from the field to the woods, and there was some threatening desultory firing on my flanks, killing one man and wounding another. After waiting thirty minutes, word was sent to the officer with the flag that the truce was granted, and that their men could come out without arms, and succor their wounded. I had no idea that the flag was properly authorized, else there would have been no firing on my flanks, but time was the precious thing I wished to gain for our trains which crowded the bottom-lands below Malvern.

My squadrons were withdrawn to the line, the infantry lay down, while officers took position in front of the line to prevent conversation with the enemy. In a few minutes thousands of men swarmed from the woods and scattered over the field. I kept myself informed by couriers of the movements of our army and trains, and had already sent officers to reassure our rear of its security, and also to bring me back a battery of artillery. Captain Frank with his battery responded. I sent a request to General Wessells, commanding Keyes's rear brigade to select a good position about two miles in my rear in case I should need a checking force when the time for withdrawal should come. That excellent soldier had already chosen such a position and established his brigade in line of battle.

When the quasi-truce had expired, at the sound of the trumpet, the line resumed its attitude of attack, and the officer with the flag again appeared with a request that the truce be extended two hours. After a reasonable wait, answer was returned that the time was extended but that no further extension would be granted. I had come on the line at 4 am, and these maneuvers and truces had consumed the time until after 9 o'clock. The Army of the Potomac was then at its new base on the James, and all its trains were safely on the way there, with Keyes's corps some miles below in my rear awaiting the enemy. So when the extended truce had expired, my command, with the exception of the cavalry, had left the field. Our dead and wounded, about 2500 in number, had been cared for during the night. Not above a dozen bodies could be found on our field during the truce, and these were buried. Twelve stalled and abandoned wagons were destroyed, and two captured guns which could not be removed were spiked and their carriages were broken. The 3rd Pennsylvania Cavalry, which had led the Army of the Potomac across White Oak Swamp, now saw its last serviceable man safe beyond Malvern Hill, before it left that glorious field, about 10 am., July 2d. A heavy rainstorm was prevailing.[17]

Somewhere on that hellish field were the remains of Private Edwin Francis Jemison, 2nd Louisiana Volunteer Infantry. He was two weeks short of being released from military service. And, he was five months short of his eighteenth birthday.

Chapter Six

HOW DID EDDIE DIE?

There is no doubt that Eddie Jemison was killed at Malvern Hill on July 1, 1862. Soon after the battle ended, his family learned the circumstances of his death. Almost certainly letters from his friends, family, and officers of the 2nd Louisiana outlining the facts of his death would have reached Monroe. Those facts have become lost over time.

A little over a month after Malvern Hill, Eddie's obituary appeared in the *Southern Recorder* (Milledgeville), written by "S," who almost certainly was his grandfather, Baradell Stubbs:

Edwin Francis Jemison, member of the 2d Regiment Louisiana Volunteers, fell in the battle of Malvern Hill, on the 1st July, 1862, aged seventeen years and seven months.

He was brave and honorable. In the first call for volunteers to defend our rights his noble and enthusiastic spirit was one of the first to respond; and nobly did he, although but a child in years, sustain himself in the front rank of the soldier and gentleman until the moment of his death. Bounding forward at the order "Charge!" he was stricken down in the front rank, and without a struggle yielded up his young life.

He was early dedicated by a loving, Christian mother, in baptism to God. May He who maketh wars to cease, comfort the sorrowing parents whose boy lies, buried by loving hands, on the battlefield near Richmond.

S.[1]

In February 1863, Eddie's aunt, his mother's younger sister, Julia Stubbs Pratt, wrote that he had been "struck down by a shell on Malvern Hill."[2]

And so matters stood, at least for the public, for over forty years. Then in 1906 the story of Eddie's death received widespread attention in the newspapers. These articles resurfaced almost one hundred years later, and the resulting information, misinformation, and mystery continues to cling to any discussion of Edwin Jemison.

On March 26, 1906, an article appeared in the *Atlanta Constitution* that describes a purported encounter between Eddie's younger brother, Robert, and a Confederate veteran by the name of Warren A. Moseley, who claimed to have witnessed Eddie's death. The article used the headline: "Soldier's Blood Spouted on Him, Captain Mosely [*sic*] Meets Brother of Wartime Comrade, While Relating the Particulars of the Killing of a Man in Battle, Dead Man's Brother Was Listening to the Story."[3]

The article reads in full:

With more than 40 years between him and the events of Malvern Hill, Capt. Warren Mosely [sic], Confederate army, was standing on the curbstone yesterday, brooding over the death of a soldier in gray, wondering who it was who stood foremost in a charge of a Louisiana brigade with fixed bayonet, advancing up the hill and across a clover patch, when a shell from a gunboat in the bay took off his head and spattered his brains and blood all about the uniform of Capt. Mosely, himself advancing through the thick rain of shot with his Georgia brigade.

"I turned suddenly at the terrible concussion caused by the proximity of the shell's trail of death," said Capt. Mosely, speaking of the incident, "and saw that man standing headless, with bayonet drawn as in the charge, his blood spurting high in the air from the jugular vein, and it seemed to me an hour before he reeled and fell still holding on to his gun. To me that was one of the most horrible sights of the period. I went back and looked at him after the fight to assure myself that it was not a dream of frenzy in those exciting moments. He was there as I had seen him fall, and more than 40 years have passed with that picture forever impressed on my memory."

Capt. Mosely was thus relating this story on the street corner to an interested party of gentlemen. He said he had long tried to learn who the private was, but while he was talking he had not noted that a listener in this group, long since the events of the civil war a gray-haired man, himself a man of those strenuous times, now growing pale and tremulous as the grim tale was reeled off. This listener then asked where the Louisiana brigade had entered the fight, and when Capt. Mosely went over this part of the story again a little chapter adding another event to the stories of the '60's was closed.

"That was my brother," said the pale man, and the one described the affair with such precision as to convince the other that they had the identical incident fastened in their minds. The interested and saddened speaker was R. W. Jemison, and it was his brother's blood that had been min-

gled with Capt. Mosely's on the uniform of the latter at
Malvern Hill when the one was killed and the other was
badly wounded in the rain of shells. Both Capt. Mosely
and Mr. Jemison have been citizens of Macon many years,
but they had not known all of this one of the many
unwritten tragedies of the civil war.

The *Atlanta Constitution* article is bylined "Constitution
Bureau, 467 Second Street, Macon, Ga, March 25 (Special)."
Obviously the story originated in Macon. A little less than a
month later, the *National Tribune* published an identical arti-
cle with the headline "His Head Blown Off, A Former
Wearer of the Gray Tells of the Tragic Death of a Comrade
During a Desperate Charge on the Union Lines at Malvern
Hill."[4] The article is prefaced with "Corporal Eugene
O'Connor, 8th GA, C.S.A., sends from Atlanta, Ga., an
account of a tragic war-time happening." It is likely that
O'Connor saw the article in the *Atlanta Constitution* and for-
warded a copy to the *National Tribune*.

Because of the stature and availability of the two newspapers, or perhaps more likely because of the gruesome nature
of the tale, this detailed and gory depiction of the death of
Eddie Jemison has become part of the lore of the young soldier.

Yet there was an earlier and much less well known account
of the death of Eddie and the meeting between Robert
Jemison, Jr. and Warren Moseley. The *Macon Telegraph* published the story ten days before the *Atlanta Constitution*'s version. The headline takes a different, and far less sanguine,
approach: "Telepathy Leads to Odd Incident, Messrs.
Moseley and Jemison Have Strange Psychic Experience
Yesterday."[5]

The article in its entirety reads:

Either telepathy or a unique coincidence has brought
to light the fact that two well-known citizens of Macon
were both deeply interested in a tragedy that occurred

Robert Jemison, Jr., Edwin's younger brother. (*Middle Georgia Archives, Washington Memorial Library, Macon, Georgia*)

Warren A. Moseley at the 1912 reunion in Macon, Georgia.
(*David N. Wiggins*)

over thirty years ago. For these two men have both lived in Macon and seen each other almost daily for much of the time that has elapsed since the tragic incident took place.

Yesterday Warren A. Moseley, the veteran police officer was standing, engrossed in deep thought, on a street corner. R.W. Jemison approached him and asked, casually, what he was thinking about. Mr. Moseley replied that he was reflecting upon an incident that took place at the battle of Malvern Hill, when he was a youth fighting under the Confederate flag.

"We were charging," he said, "when something happened that has made a profound and lifelong impression on me. A young soldier of a Louisiana regiment, which was next to mine, was shot and killed by a solid shot from a cannon, before our side had fired a shot on the charge. The young fellow's head was literally torn from his body. It was a terrible sight and the first thing of the kind I ever saw. I shall never forget it."

Mr. Jemison seemed profoundly impressed and in a voice full of emotion replied: "That man you saw killed was my brother, Edwin F. Jemison, who was killed under exactly such circumstances in the battle of Malvern Hill. I have heard his death described time and again. The man you saw shot must have been he. My brother was just 18 years of age and was a member of Company A, Second Louisiana regiment."

The two friends shook hands, feeling that the incident, which had so impressed and affected both of them, had knit them together by a stronger tie.

Those who have heard of the conversation are perplexed over the question of whether some telepathic influence, or a mere coincidence, led Mr. Jemison to inquire about the subject of Mr. Moseley's reverie.

The version of the story told by Jemison's daughter, Mamie Jemison Chestney, is very similar to the version of events reported in the *Atlanta Constitution* and the *National*

Tribune. In a family history Chestney compiled in 1964, she states: "While his [Eddie's] parents knew where he died, it was many years before they knew the details. One day my father introduced himself to a man as they sat before a hotel. The man repeated the name and said it was the first time he had heard that name since 1862; that a young soldier of that name had been fighting beside him at the Battle of Malvern Hill and been decapitated by a cannon ball. Questions proved it was Uncle Edwin."[6] Mamie Chestney apparently was not aware of the existence of the *Macon Telegraph* article. Her story may vary due to the inaccuracies of storytelling and the passage of years.

There are problems with both the *Macon Telegraph* version of the story as well as the *Constitution/Tribune* version. The *Macon Telegraph* version has the curious error of Eddie's age, as he was seventeen, not eighteen, when he was killed. The *Constitution/Tribune* rendition appears to be a grossly exaggerated and far more graphic version of that of the *Macon Telegraph,* including more alleged quotations from Warren Moseley. It even has Moseley wounded at the same time as Eddie was killed—a "fact" that appears nowhere else. At this late date it is impossible to determine if the embellished version was an enhancement made by Moseley to the *Atlanta Constitution,* something concocted by a reporter, or both. There is also the change of scene from Jemison asking Moseley what he was thinking about to one where Moseley is telling a war story on a street corner and is overheard by Jemison.

In both articles all the information about a soldier's death from a cannon ball stems from Warren Moseley himself. He cites no other witnesses. Discovering where Moseley was and what Moseley actually witnessed on July 1, 1862, Eddie's death day, is essential to finding the truth.

In 1861, Captain Moseley enlisted as a private in Company H, 4th Georgia Infantry, which was part of the Doles-Cook Brigade. The unit, known as the "Baldwin

Blues," consisted primarily of men from Baldwin County, Georgia. Milledgeville is the county seat. The 4th Georgia was sent to Virginia in the spring of 1861.

Moseley's service record indicates that he was admitted to the Regimental Hospital with "Int. Fever" on May 7, 1862, and was not returned to duty until May 18. The official record then falls silent regarding Moseley until he appears on a register of the Medical Director's Office, Richmond, as having been admitted to the hospital on October 14, 1862.[7]

Moseley's whereabouts in the late spring and summer of 1862 is critical to the story of Eddie's death, and the five-month gap in his service record between May and October needs to be accounted for to determine if he was actually at Malvern Hill. The *History of the Doles-Cook Brigade* states that he was taken prisoner at Strasburg, Virginia.[8] The *Roster of Confederate Soldiers of Georgia* is more specific, saying he was captured at Strasburg on June 1.[9]

In his 1910 Confederate Soldier's application, Moseley confirmed that he was taken prisoner "near Winchester," which is only twenty miles from Strasburg. On that application he responded to the following questions:

> Were you captured? Yes I was captured in 1862.
> Where and when? In 1862 near Winchester, Va. Sent to Point Lookout—held 3 months and exchanged.[10]

As Moseley was held prisoner for three months and was back in Confederate hands no later than October 14 when he was admitted to the hospital, he must have been captured sometime between May 19 and July 15. Perhaps he was captured on June 1 as stated in the *Roster of Confederate Soldiers of Georgia*, although that June 1 record has not been found. Realistically it appears very likely that Moseley was not present at Malvern Hill on July 1.

Even if Moseley had been at Malvern Hill, he would not have been physically close to Eddie. While the exact position on the battlefield where Eddie was killed is unknown, the movements of the 2nd Louisiana Regiment and the 4th Georgia Regiment can be traced. The extraordinary tale published in the *Atlanta Constitution* and the *National Tribune* of Moseley being covered with Eddie's blood is beyond the realm of possibility, as they were in different regiments and those regiments were separated on the battlefield. It seems this story is a case of newspapermen, or perhaps Moseley, embellishing the story.

It is also inconceivable that Moseley was able to see Eddie on the battlefield. At all times there were several regiments, thousands of men, between Eddie and Moseley. In distance they may have been separated by 400–500 yards. There was also a major battle raging. In addition, Moseley's 4th Georgia Regiment was in advance of the 2nd Louisiana on the battle-field.

Either Moseley was not at Malvern Hill or, if he was, he was not in a position to have been a witness. In any case Moseley did not see Eddie's death. Yet, in 1906 on the streets of Macon, Georgia, something clearly took place between Moseley and Robert Jemison. Sherlock Holmes said that when you have eliminated the impossible, whatever remains, *however improbable*, must be the truth. Telepathy, appearing in the *Macon Telegraph*'s tabloid-type headline, "Telepathy Leads to Odd Incident, Messers. Moseley and Jemison have Strange Psychic Experience Yesterday," is not an acceptable explanation and must fall into the impossible category, along with Moseley actually witnessing Eddie's death.

However, if Moseley actually was at Malvern Hill, what would he have been able to see? He may have seen another man, but not Eddie, get hit and killed by a projectile from a cannon. He is quoted in the *Macon Telegraph* article as saying: "A young soldier of a Louisiana regiment, which was next to mine, was shot and killed by a solid shot from a cannon, before our side had fired a shot on the charge."

A Louisiana regiment, which was next to mine. That may be the clue to the mystery. While the 2nd Louisiana Regiment, with Eddie, was a considerable distance away from the 4th Georgia, with a multitude of men between them, the 1st Louisiana Regiment was literally the next regiment to the left of the 4th Georgia Regiment. It may be that Moseley *had* seen a soldier killed in the horrific manner described in the regiment next to his own, and that he knew the regiment was from Louisiana.

Moseley may have known that Robert Jemison's brother was in a Louisiana regiment and had been killed in similar circumstances. Moseley might then have made the assumption that the man he saw killed was Robert's brother. Or, perhaps Moseley had learned something of the manner of Eddie's death in some entirely innocent fashion, perhaps many years before. Then, when the opportunity presented itself, he staged a scene in which his knowledge of Eddie's death could be viewed as supernatural, psychic, or unexplainable.

Was Moseley the sort of man who would stage a scene simply for the newspaper notoriety? Maybe. A brief look at his life is useful in evaluating Moseley as a historical witness.

Warren A. Moseley was born in South Carolina in 1838. He moved to Georgia in 1859, taking up residence in the outskirts of Milledgeville in an area that would later become known as Moseleyville. He lived about a half mile from the Stubbs residence, where Eddie Jemison lived for three years. In the small town of Milledgeville he certainly would have become familiar with the Stubbs name. No evidence has come to light suggesting that he ever met the Jemison boys when they lived nearby with their grandparents. However, it is not inconceivable.[11]

In 1860, Moseley was working as an attendant at the Georgia Lunatic Asylum in Milledgeville.[12] With the advent of war he enlisted in the Baldwin Blues. Wounded at least twice, in 1862 and 1863, he returned at the end of the war to Milledgeville and a world turned upside down.

He married in 1867 and went back to work at the asylum. In 1880, he organized a subscription to build a church. The

Moseleyville Baptist Church is still in existence although in a modern building. To supplement his income from the asylum, Moseley kept bees in 1882.[13]

The year 1882 also brought the first of many personal tragedies, when his wife of fifteen years died of consumption. Of her ten children either seven or eight survived her.[14] The following year Moseley married Fannie Summey of Stone Mountain, Georgia.[15]

Moseley helped organize the reunion of the 4th Georgia Regiment that was held in Milledgeville August 12, 1885.[16] He attended the August 25, 1886, reunion held in Talbotton, Georgia, as well.[17]

He attended the 4th Georgia Regiment event held at Oglethorpe, Georgia in July 1891.[18] In fact, his interest in the reunions seemed to have increased as time passed. Clearly he was a man who reveled in this role of aged veteran. In June 1892, he attended the 4th Georgia annual barbecue and picnic in Jeffersonville, Georgia. He wore "the coat which shows by its numerous bullet holes the number of wounds he received during the war in the service of the south."[19]

Not all activities involved veteran reunions, though. As a police officer, he was involved in solving high-profile crimes in Macon, including the capture of an escaped murderer in 1892, for which he received a "big reward."[20] The police chief, John T. Boisfeuillet (who was Robert Jemison's brother-in-law), was thinking of resigning. Moseley was one of those who signed a petition asking him to stay on.[21] Although he was almost seventy years old in 1907, Moseley ran unsuccessfully for chief of police.[22]

He went to the reunion in August 1893 in Talbotton.[23] At the 1894 reunion in Milledgeville Moseley not only attended but "has in his possession about $18,000 of Confederate money, and every four or five years pays the boys off, which is a sweet memento of old times."[24] Naturally, he attended the 1895 reunion as well.[25]

Moseley was a great storyteller. One tale, printed in various newspapers in December 1900, describes a strange incident involving a "Hoodoo hat" which Moseley related at the Augusta, Georgia, reunion. The story goes that at the "battle of Winchester" a Union soldier was shot through the head, the bullet passing through his hat. A soldier of the 4th Georgia, the same regiment Moseley was in, saw the hat and picked it up and wore it. "He had not had it on his head for more than two hours when he was shot through the head, the bullet piercing the hat in almost the same hole that the bullet had entered that killed the Yankee." Despite two men having been killed by shots through the hat, another 4th Georgia soldier picked up the hat and he too was struck in the head with an enemy bullet. Yet another 4th Georgia soldier picked up the hat and was shot in the head the following day. The 4th Georgia soldiers who allegedly had worn the "hoodoo hat" were all named in the article. The tale relates that this hat, despite having four previous wearers shot through the head, was still "a fine one," but no one would pick it up again and it was left on the field. While this is a curious tale its publication also marks the first time in print that Moseley was styled as "Captain."[26]

Moseley also used his status as a Confederate veteran to make some extra money. In newspapers across the country in 1904 and 1905 an advertisement appeared featuring two "famous Confederate Veterans," along with their photographs, who "use and recommend" Duffy's Pure Malt Whiskey. One of the "famous veterans" was "Captain Warren Moseley," who is quoted as saying, "I never felt better in my life, and I owe it all to Duffy's Pure Malt Whiskey. I was wounded eight times during the war and after General Lee's surrender returned home completely broken down. My wounds gave me a good deal of trouble, and I had attacks of extreme weakness, with great loss of blood. Doctors said nothing would enrich my blood and build me up so quickly and thoroughly as Duffy's Pure Malt Whiskey. I took nothing else. Although past 65, I am in perfect physical and mental condition and devote twelve hours a day to my business."

The advertisement is endorsed by Warren A. Moseley, 320 Columbus St., Macon, Ga., July 23, 1904.[27] Moseley probably considered the ad a way to raise some much needed cash. Moseley's 1910 Confederate Soldier's Pension application states that he possessed no assets of value of any kind. He stated that his only income was $70 per month working for the City of Macon.[28] No matter what the reasoning behind the advertisement, the content of the ad does damage his credibility as an accurate storyteller unless, of course, Duffy's Pure Malt Whiskey did restore his health.

In November 1905, there was a large reunion in Macon. Moseley was in charge of the cavalry. He encouraged old veterans, as well as sons of veterans, to participate. His intention was to have five hundred cavalrymen in attendance. The newspapers touted that the parade would feature a cavalry charge and that "the fact that Captain Moseley will be in charge is assurance of a most interesting affair. This veteran was engaged in nineteen battles, and was wounded eight times. He will wear a uniform which he possessed during the war."[29]

When the parade was over, "Moseley and his cavalrymen formed at the foot of Cherry Street [Macon, Georgia] and charged up to Cotton Avenue. All the old men in this troop rode as in their younger days, and they seemed to warm up to that rugged heat of excitement always evident among the men on the eve of battle. The war whoop sounded and the men were off. At breakneck speed, they dashed down the paved street, flashing old-time sabers. The crowds fell in behind them and yelled themselves hoarse."[30]

It was four months later, March 16, 1906, that the peculiar sidewalk meeting between Robert Jemison, Jr. and Warren Moseley took place in Macon where Moseley gave his alleged eyewitness account of Eddie's death. The local, state, and national coverage of that incident may have helped bolster his stature for his next veteran activity. This time it would be a reunion from all the former Confederate states and was to be held in Richmond, Virginia.

Moseley had become something of a local celebrity as he basked in the glory of being an old veteran. In preparation for the May 1907 reunion Moseley was appointed to the staff of a General A. J. West as part of the Georgia contingent. The *Atlanta Constitution* carried the story along with a photograph.[31]

> Captain Warren Moseley of Macon . . . is among the few very striking typical Confederate soldiers left to enjoy the annual reunions. He entered the war as a private in the 4th regiment Georgia volunteers, from Milledgeville, was engaged in nineteen battles and skirmishes, wounded eight times during the war, was a prisoner many times, and as often exchanged. He was given a captain's commission by Governor Joseph E. Brown and toward the end of the war operated in north Georgia and Tennessee where bushwhackers were fought. Moseley has since the war been a citizen of Macon and has served on the Macon police force for a long period. His devotion to the veterans' reunion and the commemoration of the courage and bravery of southern soldiers make him at once a loyal Confederate.

The *Atlanta Constitution* carried several articles on the Richmond Confederate veterans' reunion. In the first there is a long quote from Moseley:

> At that time the ladies of this city gave several church bells in order that they might be broken up and used to make cannon for the confederate army. There was enough metal in the bells to make three cannon. About twenty-five pounds were left, and the remainder was used in making buckles for the soldiers' belts. These latter contained the letters "C.S."

We were then operating in the valley of Virginia. I wear today the same pair of trousers I had on when I was wounded in the thigh and leg. I was also wounded several other times.

I have not been here in forty-four years. I went down to the battlefield of Seven Pines yesterday, where our brigade first went into the fight. I went to King's school house, near Frayser's farm, where I found a house from which we fought full of bullet holes. I then went down to the swamp and found twelve pounds of shot and shell. I also found a broken sabre, which was evidently broken over the head of one of the enemy."[32]

The next article about Moseley and the reunion in Richmond appeared a few days later when Moseley, "covered with reunion medals, flags and other decorations . . . returned from Richmond," stopped over for a few hours in Atlanta. "Over forty years ago, I saw a saber broken over the head of a union soldier. I went back to that spot a few days ago and found a piece of the same weapon," said Moseley as he displayed his trophy.[33]

Moseley apparently had collected a large number of relics from the war and was said to have "one of the most complete museums in the state."[34] In August 1907 he was given a photograph by a Union veteran of "the Frazur house" taken shortly "after the battle of Seven Pines." Moseley commented that he remembered the house well as he and three other members of the 4th Georgia defended the house. The four, he said, killed more than eighty of the enemy.

After so many years the old veteran can be forgiven if he got his battles and geography confused. Perhaps it was another house. If he was referring to the fighting at Frazier's Farm (also known as Glendale) on June 30, 1862, he is mistaken, as the 4th Georgia did not see action there.[35]

A brief look at the history of Warren Moseley may not be enough to categorically answer the question as to whether or not he was capable of staging an event to entrap Robert Jemison with information about the death of Eddie. Moseley was a great storyteller and clearly loved an audience. Did Jemison or Moseley go to the office of the *Macon Telegraph* and report the incident? As Moseley was frequently in the newspapers and Jemison was almost never in the press, it seems likely that if one of them did bring the peculiar incident to the *Macon Telegraph* it was probably Moseley. The fact that the *Macon Telegraph* article quotes Jemison and mentions the detail that Eddie had been in the 2nd Louisiana opens the possibility that they both went to the newspaper. Or Jemison could have mentioned the 2nd Louisiana to Moseley, who then took that fact to the paper. We will never know.

What we know as fact is that by sundown July 1, 1862, Eddie was dead. As Sherlock Holmes instructs, we can eliminate Moseley seeing Eddie on the battlefield because Moseley either was not present or, if present, was not physically able to see Eddie. We can also eliminate the mental telepathy suggestion made by the headline of the *Macon Telegraph* as impossible.

We still have a couple of theories that are more likely than improbable. To summarize, Julia Stubbs Pratt wrote that Eddie was killed by a "shell." This is at least the story being told within the family in the months after his death. The Confederates suffered a huge number of casualties from cannon fire, which makes the claim of his being killed by a cannon shell more likely. In addition, Robert Jemison volunteered that the death Moseley described in the *Macon Telegraph* article (not the *Atlanta Constitution/Tribune* articles) fit the death of Eddie, a story he had heard "time and again." Therefore, if the death Moseley described was either that which he saw of a man in the 1st Louisiana or a story he had heard about Eddie, it was close enough that Jemison accepted that it was Eddie.

Did Eddie lose his head to a shell? Probably. However, the definitive answer is unknowable. Only the theories can be weighed for value and the final determination left to the individual to judge.

Chapter Seven

"PEACE TO HIS ASHES"

On a warm April day, 140 years after Eddie Jemison was killed, a small group of people gathered around an obelisk standing in Memory Hill Cemetery in Milledgeville. Adults and children alike were in attendance, with one woman dressed in Civil War era widow's weeds. She was not the only one in period dress. Nine men dressed as Confederate soldiers carrying the battle flag of the Army of Northern Virginia marched into the lot as a unit and fired a volley. It was Confederate Memorial Day in Georgia, and the Sons of Confederate Veterans were there to honor Eddie with the unveiling of a new monument to the young soldier they thought was buried in the family plot of his grandfather,

Baradell Stubbs.[1] The monument is small, low to the ground, and made of granite. In addition to his name, regiment, and the years he lived, it bears the famous photograph of Eddie and the inscription: "A young man who placed his loyalty to the cause above his own life."

This monument was not the first placed there to commemorate Eddie. There is also a short marble monument, two inches thick and twelve and a half inches wide, with a rounded top bearing the inscription "E.F. Jemison, 2nd La. Vols." This monument was placed by citizens of Milledgeville in 1896 during a massive effort to mark all the graves in Memory Hill of the men who had been Confederate soldiers. The local newspaper carried articles soliciting the public for the names of servicemen for the marking project, and as a result, several hundred markers were placed in the cemetery. No one needed to come forward to provide information on Eddie, as his name and service were clearly marked on a tall marble obelisk standing in the Stubbs family plot, the first monument erected bearing Eddie's name.[2] It is these two earlier monuments, especially the obelisk, that have led people to believe that Eddie was buried at Memory Hill. People assume that because there is a marker for him, Eddie must be there.

However, one must keep in mind that having a name carved on stone in a cemetery does not necessarily mean that the remains of the deceased are there. Often stones are placed as monuments to the memory of a person rather than to mark the actual gravesite. In the case of the obelisk, it appears to be a marker commemorating Eddie's short life.

The obelisk carries two names on it, Eddie's and that of his elder brother Henry, who died in November 1859. Whether Henry had a tombstone or wooden marker placed on the grave at that time is not known; however, it is the only marker for him now, and it is clear that the obelisk was not put up at the time of his death. Opposite sides of the obelisk have intricate designs that include both Henry's and Eddie's information in a planned arrangement. Most important, the obelisk's west side has "Edwin and Henry" carved on a shield in relief that was cut from the same continuous piece of stone as the rest of the obelisk. It was not carved separately and then attached at a later date. Eddie's name being the first listed is a clear indication that the obelisk was erected sometime after Eddie's death in 1862, not after Henry's death in 1859.

However it is not possible to establish exactly when after 1862 it was erected. A rough estimation can be made from the inscription of the stone carver's name at the base of the monument: "J. Artope & Son, Macon." While there are many monuments made by the Artope company, the only monuments in Memory Hill that have the company name inscribed exactly this way bear death dates from the 1860s on. Moreover, the Macon City Directory listed the company as "J. Artope & Son" between 1860 and 1872. By 1877, the company was listed as "Tom B. Artope."[3] With this information it can safely be assumed that the obelisk was carved between Eddie's death in 1862 and 1877.[4]

Since only the obelisk was placed near the time of Eddie's death, the question to ask now is: is Eddie buried under the obelisk, or is he lying in an unmarked grave at Malvern Hill?

It was certainly possible for a soldier to be killed in Virginia, or elsewhere, in July 1862 and have the remains buried in Georgia. In fact, Milledgeville's first battle casualty of the war, killed at Pensacola on November 20, 1861, was returned to Milledgeville and buried ten days after his death.[5]

There are also instances of bodies being retrieved from distant battlefields and returned after the war. In 1866, the remains of a soldier killed in November 1863 at Knoxville, Tennessee, were returned to Milledgeville.[6] Disinterring a body, though, must have been extremely unpleasant. The number of those killed, decomposition, and battle injuries would have made body identification horrific and close to impossible. Despite these obstacles, it was done. Whether prior to or after burial, once a body was recovered, it required transportation to its final destination. Six weeks after Malvern Hill an article appeared in a Macon newspaper vividly describing the difficulties involved and suggesting a potential solution: "Our [the newspaper editors'] attention was called particularly to this subject, while on a visit to our Cemetery one day last week. A body had been brought here by railroad, we believe, from Atlanta, on its way to Dooly County, and had become so offensive that further transportation was refused. After remaining at the depot some time, a guard was detailed from Col. Brown's encampment for that purpose and the body buried."[7]

The editors of the newspaper article quoted from an article in the *Richmond Dispatch and Whig* newspaper:

> We daily observe at the railway stations boxes containing the bodies of deceased soldiers, which have been disinterred by their friends, under the belief that they can be sent off without delay either by mail train or express. This, however, is an error. Freight trains only carry them, and the detention frequently causes the bodies to become offensive, when their immediate burial by the wayside is a matter of necessity. It would be better to postpone disinterment until cold weather, when it can be accomplished with less trouble and more certainty of getting the remains of the departed to their destination. Metallic coffins are difficult to obtain, and wooden ones can only be procured by the payment of a large sum. In these the dead bodies are packed with sawdust, and in warm weather their transportation to a distant point is uncertain, if not absolutely impossible.

The Macon newspaper editors disagreed with these observations and conclusions. They suggested another method of transporting the dead: "To the above we have to add, (and that from personal knowledge) that nothing is more easy, convenient, or cheap than transporting bodies at any season of the year, to any distance. Any common coffin will answer. Have a piece of cotton osnaburgs or other cloth of the necessary size—dip it in boiling tar, and wrap the coffin in it and it is sealed tighter than it can be done in a metallic case. Place it in a box with some kind of packing to keep it from moving, and the work is complete. No charcoal, or disinfectant is necessary."[8]

While it was possible to move the remains of deceased soldiers immediately after death, or even after the passage of several years, the question remains as to whether or not Eddie's remains were ever moved to Milledgeville. To help answer that question, a thorough search of the Milledgeville newspapers was made and produced no indication that Eddie's remains were ever returned. It is not surprising, considering the conditions under which the fallen at Malvern Hill were buried. The day after the battle, both the Confederate and Union armies returned to the battlefield to bury their dead. Thousands of corpses lay before them in the pouring rain. Graves had to be dug through mud, and no doubt it was done as quickly as possible.

Although no documents exist that record the exact details of Eddie's burial, there are two very important documents that tell us he was buried at Malvern Hill. One is his obituary. During the Civil War, the Milledgeville newspapers published few obituaries. Those that they did publish generally were short, and most were for officers. Therefore, it is somewhat surprising to find an obituary, and a long one, for Eddie. After all, he was only a private and did not live in Milledgeville for long. Most likely it was the influence of his grandfather, Baradell Stubbs that allowed Eddie an obituary. The obituary states, "May He who maketh wars to cease, comfort the sorrowing parents whose boy lies, buried by loving hands, on the battlefield near Richmond."[9]

The second document was written seven months after Eddie's death. His maternal aunt, Julia Pratt, wrote in a letter that Eddie and "his intimate friend and mate" were both killed at Malvern Hill and "they sleep side by side buried on the battlefield, their graves rudely marked by comrades, who buried them."[10]

There is little doubt that Eddie was initially buried at Malvern Hill by the men with whom he fought. Is it possible, though, that his body was later retrieved and then reinterred underneath the obelisk at Memory Hill? Such a burial is highly unlikely, and to understand why, one has to examine the Stubbs's family plot.

During this time period it was customary in Memory Hill Cemetery to build a brick vault inside the grave. The casket was not simply placed in a hole in the ground, but rather the casket was placed into a brick structure built below ground that had walls, but no floor. The brick vault was the length of the grave and about three feet wide. The top was a brick arch that comes almost to the surface of the ground. A marble or brick slab, called a "ledger,"[11] was placed on the surface of the ground to act as a capstone, adding strength to the vault. After the burial service the casket would be lowered into the unfinished vault. The brick mason would then construct the vaulted roof. There is no door or opening; the entire structure is underground and sealed with brick and mortar. The view from the surface is of the ledger with no indication that there is a brick vault beneath it. There are hundreds of such below-the-ground, and invisible, brick vaults in Memory Hill Cemetery.

The size of the vault can be easily determined by sticking a thin metal probe, such as a long thin screwdriver, into the ground around the ledger in order to feel the edges of the vault. The vault under the obelisk bearing the names of Henry and Eddie appears to be of normal size for one burial. And with a vault in place for Henry, there would be no room to place a second body. However, there is the question of whether or not Eddie's remains could have been buried alongside the ledger bearing the obelisk. The grave to the north side of the Jemison obelisk was already used when Henry died in 1859. It is the location of the remains of Robert Small Pratt, one of Eddie's cousins, who died in 1857. His was the first burial in the Stubbs lot.

Jemison monument in the Stubbs's family plot at Memory Hill Cemetery, Milledgeville, Georgia. (*Hugh T. Harrington*)

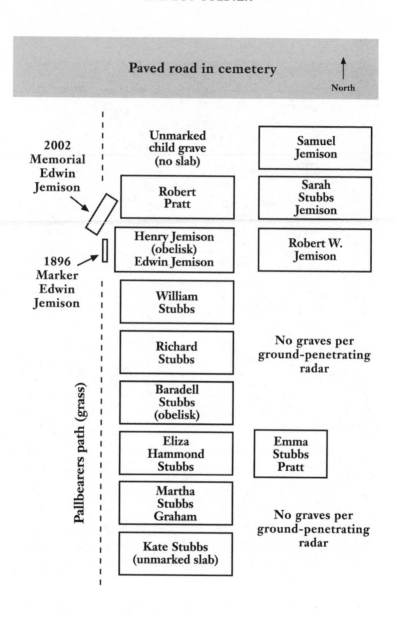

Plan of the Stubbs family plot at Memory Hill Cemetery, Milledgeville, Georgia.

To the west of the obelisk is a pallbearer's path running through the cemetery. There are no graves along the path.

To the south of the obelisk is the grave of William B. Stubbs who died in 1864. Had Eddie been brought back before 1864, it is likely this spot would have been his.

To the east of the obelisk is the grave of Eddie's father, Robert Jemison who died in 1879. Clearly, Eddie could not be buried there, either.

There is a grave location to the north of the grave of Robert Small Pratt (two graves to the north of the Jemison obelisk) that from the surface appears not to have been used. Discreet poking with a small probe reveals bricks just under the surface. In the 1930s, when the cemetery was first indexed, this grave was described as being that of a child.[12]

There are also several grave sites in the lot that appear not to have been used for burials. Probing does not indicate there are bricks below the surface of the ground on any of them. The cemetery was surveyed in 2012 with ground-penetrating radar specifically searching for burial sites that are not marked or visible above ground. The ground-penetrating radar did not discover burials in any of the unmarked locations in this lot.[13]

It seems likely that if Eddie had been reinterred in Memory Hill, his parents would have given him his own monument, rather than have both Eddie's and Henry's names carved onto the monument atop Henry's grave. The obelisk with the brothers' names has loving inscriptions on it to Eddie. The one from his father reads, in Latin, "Sweet is the reward for those who die for their country." His mother's, in English, describes Eddie as "A more dutiful son never lived. A braver soldier never died. Peace to his ashes."[14] How could parents not have put those sentiments on a separate monument if their son was buried on this lot? Despite losing much in the war, the Jemisons could certainly afford a separate monument for Eddie.

While Memory Hill Cemetery is a beautiful and peaceful place, and it is pleasant to think of Eddie at rest among his family, the facts do not bear out that conclusion. Rather, the facts point to Eddie's remains not being moved at any time to Memory Hill.

After the war, massive efforts were made by the federal government to move Union dead from battlefield graves to national cemeteries. Similar efforts were made by southerners for the Confederate dead. The Ladies' Memorial Associations and similar organizations moved tens of thousands of Confederate dead from battlefields. However, these removal projects did not include the battlefield at Malvern Hill. The Confederate dead at Malvern Hill were, generally speaking, not buried where they fell but were removed from the farm fields and buried in nearby wooded areas by Confederate forces after the battle. In the decades after the war when a grave was uncovered, the remains were often removed to Hollywood Cemetery in Richmond. These occurrences were few in number. Robert E. L. Krick, historian at Richmond National Battlefield Park, wrote, "Private Jemison's remains most likely are at Malvern Hill."[15]

It is entirely reasonable to accept the evidence, and also the view that the family would not interfere with the remains of Eddie and his friend who "sleep side by side buried on the battlefield." They sleep there still.

NOTES ON SELECT
PRINCIPAL PARTICIPANTS

CHESTNEY, MAMIE JEMISON (December 12, 1874–June 27, 1970): She was the daughter of Robert W. Jemison, Jr. and Kate Loring Boisfeuillet. She wrote the Jemison genealogy *Skeletons of the History of the Jemison and Boisfeuillet Families* (Macon: privately printed, 1964). She never identified Warren Moseley as the man behind the disturbing newspaper articles that appeared in 1906 concerning her Uncle Edwin's death at Malvern Hill. It is ironic that Moseley's grave is only one hundred feet away from her own grave in Rose Hill Cemetery, Macon, Georgia. Mamie Jemison Chestney's grave is at: Latitude: 32.84654167°, Longitude: -83.63306389°.

FORT, TOMLINSON (July 14, 1787–May 11, 1859): Dr. Fort is buried in the Fort plot in Memory Hill Cemetery, Milledgeville, Georgia. West side, section E, lot 52, Latitude: 33.07492550°, Longitude: -83.22963305°.

JEMISON, EDWIN FRANCIS (December 1, 1844–July 1, 1862): Eddie's name appears on the shared obelisk with his brother

Henry in the Stubbs plot in Memory Hill Cemetery, Milledgeville, Georgia. East side, section F, lot 26, Latitude: 33.07530833°, Longitude: -83.22836919°. Eddie is buried in an unknown location on the battlefield at Malvern Hill, Virginia.

JEMISON, HENRY BARADELL (March 4, 1843–November 4, 1859): Eddie's brother Henry is buried in the Stubbs plot in Memory Hill Cemetery, Milledgeville, Georgia. His name appears on the shared obelisk with his brother Edwin. East side, section F, lot 26.

JEMISON, OWEN FORT (c. 1846–January 2, 1906): Eddie's younger brother moved to New Orleans where he worked as a clerk. He married Mary McConnell in 1875, and sometime in the early 1890s they moved to New York City where they raised Owen's nephew Richard. After Mary's death in 1902, Owen went back to New Orleans where he lived until his death on January 2, 1906. He was killed by a train while crossing Canal Street at St. Charles. He was buried in New Orleans, the exact location unknown.

JEMISON, ROBERT SR. AND SARAH: Eddie's parents remained in Monroe with their three surviving sons until after the war. In 1870 they moved back to Macon, where Robert practiced law with his stepfather, Samuel B. Hunter. The causes are unknown, but on January 17, 1879, Robert shot and killed himself in the apartment where he lived with Sarah. He was fifty-eight years old at the time of his death. Sarah lived another sixteen years spending her time visiting with friends and family. She died in Macon on October 22, 1894, a year after suffering a stroke from which she never recovered.[1] They are buried in the Stubbs family plot at Memory Hill Cemetery in Milledgeville, Georgia. The gravestone for Eddie's father bears the wrong death date. It bears the date of July 17, 1878. Actually, Robert Jemison, Sr. died January 17, 1879.[2] His obituary is remarkably detailed. The erroneous death date apparently came from the genealogy written by Mamie Jemison Chestney, Robert Jemison Jr.'s daughter. In her genealogy she quotes and paraphrases from the obituary, but used the wrong date.

JEMISON, ROBERT JR. (April 24, 1848–September 3, 1929): When he was just sixteen years old, as his brother Eddie did before him, young Robert enlisted in the Confederate army. He was a private in the 6th Texas Cavalry, Company A, from February 1865 until the war ended two months later. He was assigned to a recruiting squad. However, the war ended before he could join his unit.[3] After the war, he moved to Macon, where he married Kate Loring Boisfeuillet in 1873. Together, they had six children, five of whom survived to adulthood. Robert worked for the railroad, which took the family all across the South. By 1886, when his youngest son Richard was born, Robert and his family had settled back in Macon. Kate died in the weeks after Richard's birth, leaving Robert a widower. Five years later, he married Lannie Holt Holmes. Their daughter Roberta was born in 1892; however, she died just four years later. Robert worked as a bookkeeper until his retirement in 1921. He died in 1929, and Lannie followed nine years later. They are buried together, with their daughter Roberta, at Rose Hill Cemetery in Macon. Inexplicably, in about 2008 a Veterans Administration Confederate grave marker appeared on Robert Jemison's grave bearing the inscription for Sgt. John C. Holmes, Co. D, 45 Ga. Inf. 1836–Feb. 3, 1869. Grave location: Latitude: 32.84791667°, Longitude: -83.63315°.

JEMISON, SAMUEL (May 17, 1852–December 21, 1886): Eddie's brother Samuel left home at eighteen to attend college at Washington College (now known as Washington & Lee University) in Virginia. After graduation he studied law in Monroe under the tutelage of his uncle, Frank Stubbs. After being admitted into the bar, Sam relocated to Macon, where he entered into practice with his father. After his father's death, Sam continued to practice law and was known to be distinguished in this position. In December 1886, while defending a client in court, Sam fell dangerously ill. He died just before dawn on December 21, just thirty-four years old. He is buried with his family in the Stubbs plot at Memory Hill Cemetery in Milledgeville.[4]

MAGRUDER, JOHN BANKHEAD (May 1, 1807–February 18, 1871): After the Seven Days battles, Lee reorganized his army. General Magruder was reassigned to command the district of Texas, New Mexico, and Arizona. On January 1, 1863, he won the battle of Galveston. After the war he went to Mexico where he was a major general in the Imperial Mexican army. He died in Houston, Texas, and is buried in the Trinity Episcopal Cemetery in Galveston. Latitude: 29.2936611°, Longitude: -94.8112335°.

MOSELEY, WARREN A. (1838–December 17, 1912): Warren Moseley, the Confederate veteran and police officer who gloried in all things concerning the war and his service, died in poverty at 330 Columbus Street in Macon. He was buried in Rose Hill Cemetery in Macon, Georgia. After decades of promoting his veteran status he does not have a grave marker indicating Confederate service. His grave is located at: Latitude: 32.84624167°, Longitude: -83.63298056°.

PURVIS, GEORGE SR.: George Purvis worked alongside Robert Jemison in the land office until December 1862. In the early morning hours of the 11th, George's house was consumed by fire. George sustained terrible burns while trying to rescue his family. Four of his six children and their nurse died in the fire. George died the next day from his injuries.

STUBBS, BARADELL AND ELIZA: After the war Baradell and Eliza sold their Midway home and moved to Savannah, where they lived with their daughter Emma and her family as well as their children, Kate and Richard. Shortly after Richard's death in 1871 they moved to Macon to live with

Sarah and Robert Jemison. On October 17, 1873, Baradell died "after a painful and protracted illness at the advanced age of 74 years, 8 months and 14 days."[5] Eliza followed on November 1, 1889. Her funeral service was in the Presbyterian church in Milledgeville where she was one of the original members in 1825.[6] They are both buried in the Stubbs plot at Memory Hill Cemetery, Milledgeville, Georgia.

STUBBS, CATHERINE "KATE" (November 22, 1832–May 9, 1918): Eddie's aunt Kate spent the years between the end of the war and her death living with various family members in Savannah, Louisiana, and Macon. She never married. She is buried in the Stubbs plot in Memory Hill Cemetery beneath an unmarked slab.

STUBBS, ELLEN (1843–February 15, 1918): Eddie's aunt Ellen married Joseph King on May 29, 1861, in Milledgeville. Together they had seven children, the eldest of whom was named Edwin in memory of her nephew and friend. Eddie King was a contractor and important founder of Fort Lauderdale, Florida. This namesake of Eddie died September 16, 1928, in the Okeechobee Hurricane near Lake Okeechobee, Florida. Edwin King had a son, Edwin Byrd King, on December 5, 1887. This Edwin, the last of the family to be named Edwin, died February 29, 1980, and is buried in Evergreen Cemetery, Fort Lauderdale, Florida. Ellen had another son named in honor of her brother Richard. After spending time in Georgia, Ellen and Joseph eventually settled in Florida, first Volusia County and then Broward County. Ellen died on February 15, 1918, eight months after Joseph.

STUBBS, EMMA (March 15, 1846–July 7, 1916): Two years after the war, Eddie's aunt Emma married Charles Pratt (May 15, 1867). Charles was the younger brother of Nathanial Pratt, who was married to Emma's sister Julia. Emma and

Charles, with their children, moved across Georgia, first to Savannah with Emma's family, then to Hancock County, and finally to Atlanta. They had six children. She died of pneumonia and is buried in the Stubbs plot in Memory Hill Cemetery, Milledgeville, Georgia. East side, section F, lot 26.

STUBBS, FRANK (1832–May 1, 1908): After resigning his commission as first lieutenant in the Pelican Grays, Eddie's uncle Frank returned to Monroe. The following year he was commissioned as a second lieutenant in Madison Light Artillery where he served until May 1864. At war's end he continued to practice law and served a term as a state senator. Frank was married twice, first to Margaret Linton, with whom he had a son, and then, following Margaret's death, to Georgia Tucker. Frank and Georgia had sixteen children, six of whom did not live to adulthood. Evidence of the Stubbs family can still be seen in Monroe today (Stubbs Avenue, Georgia Tucker Elementary School—now abandoned). Georgia died in 1904 at the age of fifty-six, and Frank died on May 1, 1908, at the age of seventy-six.

STUBBS, JULIA (December 20, 1834–April 16, 1907): Eddie's aunt Julia married Nathaniel Pratt on November 14, 1855. Nathaniel was the older brother of Charles Pratt, who was married to Julia's sister Emma. Julia named a son Henry Jemison Pratt after her nephew. Henry Jemison Pratt (April 29, 1860–October 7, 1890) died in Rome, Georgia, and is buried in Decatur Cemetery, Decatur, Georgia. Julia is buried in the same cemetery.

STUBBS, LOUISA (June 6, 1837–1890): In December 1858 Eddie's aunt Louisa married William Hurt Harris, a doctor and Oglethorpe University graduate. They lived in the Midway area after their wedding, but eventually moved to Hancock County, Georgia, where William was from. Over the course of the years Louisa's mother lived with them and their children as well as her sisters Kate and Emma (with

Emma's family). Louisa died in 1890 and William the following year. They are buried in Oak Grove Cemetery in Brunswick, Georgia.

STUBBS, MARIA (1825–1853): Eddie's aunt married an Episcopal minister, Reverend William Flinn. They relocated to Demopolis, Alabama, where they had three children. Only one, Sarah Jemison Flinn, lived to adulthood. Maria died in 1853. William Flinn remarried and returned to Milledgeville. He became the chaplain of the 4th Georgia Regiment and would have known Warren Moseley. Sarah Jemison Flinn lived in New Orleans and later St. Louis where she died in 1913.

STUBBS, MARTHA (1828–December 21, 1910): Eddie's aunt married Presbyterian minister Arthur Small. Prior to 1860 they had relocated to Alabama, where Arthur died in 1865. Two years later Martha married Chancellor Smith Graham. Martha moved to Vicksburg where she died. She is buried in the Stubbs plot in Memory Hill Cemetery, Milledgeville, Georgia. East side, section F, lot 26.

STUBBS, RICHARD NICHOLS (May 23, 1849–November 15, 1871): Eddie's uncle died in Savannah, Georgia, of "conjestive fever."[7] He is buried in the Stubbs plot in Memory Hill Cemetery, Milledgeville, Georgia. East side, section F, lot 26.

STUBBS, WILLIAM "WILLIE" BARADELL (June 15, 1840–July 17, 1864): Eddie's Uncle Willie was discharged from the Pelican Grays in 1862. He returned to his father's home in Midway. There, he became a part of Company H, 9th State Troops. In 1864 he fell ill, and succumbed to his sickness on July 17. Willie is buried in the Stubbs lot, Memory Hill Cemetery, Milledgeville, Georgia. East side, section F, lot 26.

NOTES

INTRODUCTION

1. *The American Heritage Picture History of the Civil War* (New York: American Heritage Publishing Company, 1960) 61.
2. *Union Recorder* (Milledgeville, Ga.), May 26, 1996, 13A.
3. *Union Recorder* (Milledgeville, Ga.), May 26, 1996, 13A.
4. Sarah Stubbs Jemison, the mother of Edwin Jemison, was a daughter of Baradell and Eliza Stubbs. The children who lived in the Stubbs home were also children of Baradell and Eliza Stubbs. Therefore, despite their young ages these children would be the aunts and uncles of Eddie Jemison.

CHAPTER ONE: IN THE BEGINNING

1. *Georgia Telegraph* (Macon, Ga.), April 27, 1847.
2. Alan P. Tankersley, *College Life at Old Oglethorpe* (Athens: University of Georgia Press, 1951), 5. *Southern Recorder* (Milledgeville, Ga.), November 23, 1847.
3. *Georgia Telegraph*, October 12, 1847, 3.
4. Robert Jemison, Jr. would be born April 24, 1847, in Jackson Parish, Louisiana.
5. Biographical and History Memoirs of Louisiana, vol. 1 (Chicago: Chicago Publishing Company, 1892), 412.
6. The 79.5 acres was located along what is now Robinson Chapel Road, near Louisiana Highway 144. Certificate #9243.
7. There does not appear to be any trace of the Jemison house or any buildings that were part of the plantation extant.
8. Midway is a mile south of Milledgeville, the former capital of Georgia (1804–1868).

9. The house still stands today. The Stubbs house is located on South Wayne Street (business route 441). It is a private residence.

10. The initials "RNS" on the window pane had long lost their meaning. In 2002, the identification of "Richard Nichols Stubbs" (1849–1871), son of Baradell and Eliza (Hammond) Stubbs, was made by author Alexandra Filipowski.

11. As late as 2002 old newspapers still covered the walls in the attic rooms acting as insulation for warmth on cold winter nights.

12. Baradell and Eliza had two daughters, Maria and Martha, who had relocated to Alabama. Maria died there in 1853.

13. *Catalogue of the Officers, Alumni & Students of Oglethorpe University 1857–1858* (Macon, Ga.: Lewis H. Andrews, 1858). Oglethorpe University had stiff entrance requirements. Its catalog declared that "Candidates for the Freshman Class are examined in Caesar, Cicero's Select Orations, Virgil, Sallust, Greek Testament (John's Gospel), Graeca Minora or Greek Reader, English Grammar, Geography and Arithmetic."

14. Daniel Walker Howe, "Classical Education in America," *Wilson Quarterly*, Spring, 2011.

15. Charles was the son of Charles Hammond and Evaline (Harris) Hammond. John was the son of John Hammond and Caroline (Fort) Hammond. Both were grandsons of Abner Hammond making them Richard's first cousins, and Eddie and Henry first cousins once removed. John was also Eddie and Henry's second cousin through the Fort line on their father's side.

16. Dr. Fort's home originally stood at the northeast corner of South Liberty and Greene streets. In the twentieth century it was moved to its current location at 311 South Liberty Street. It is a private residence.

17. Dr. Tomlinson Fort, July 14, 1787–May 11, 1859. Eddie would have seen Dr. Fort's body on Wednesday, May 11, then attended the funeral at 4 p.m. the following day.

18. While they were in combat in 1812 these men were not part of the War of 1812, which was against Great Britain. Their war, the Patriot War, was an undeclared war between the United States and Spain over Spanish East Florida. Almost unknown today, the Patriot War was a political and military fiasco for the United States.

19. The road was east of I-95, exit 323.

20. Tomlinson Fort's grave is located on the West side, section E, Lot 52, grave 10, 33.07492550 Latitude, -83.22963305 Longitude.

21. William Flinn (1818–1897) was Eddie's uncle by marriage through his deceased maternal aunt Maria Stubbs Finn.

22. *Southern Recorder* (Milledgeville, Ga.) and *Federal Union* (Milledgeville, Ga.), May 17, 1859.

23. The specific nature of his injury is not known.

24. Eddie's cousin one-year-old Robert Small Pratt died on September 2, 1857. He was the son of Nathaniel and Julia (Stubbs) Pratt. Young Robert was the first family member to be buried in the Stubbs plot in the City Cemetery now known as Memory Hill Cemetery.

25. US Census, 1860. Scottsboro District, Baldwin County, Ga. After Henry's funeral there is no evidence of Eddie's whereabouts. In all likelihood, he finished out the school year. By early July 1860 Eddie was no longer living with his grandfather in Milledgeville.

26. Frank Stubbs taught school for several years until deciding to persue a career in law. He was admitted to the bar in October 1851.

27. The sister-in-law and nephew of George Purvis also lived with the Purvis family.

CHAPTER TWO: ENLISTMENT TO MARCH 1862

1. *Ouachita Telegraph* (Monroe, La.), September 19, 1885, 3.

2. Terry G. Scriber, *Twenty-Seventh Louisiana Volunteer Infantry* (Gretna, La.: Pelican Publishing Company, 2006). *A Short History of Camp Moore*, accessed January 2, 2015, http://www.camp-moorela.com/.

3. *A Short History of Camp Moore*, accessed January 2, 2015, http://www.campmoorela.com/.

4. Willie Stubbs relocated to Monroe sometime between late October 1860 and April 1861, according to the 1860 US Census.

5. *Monroe Morning World* (Monroe, La.), "Little Red Brick House Showplace for its Historical Items," December 11, 1966, 31.

6. *Colfax Chronicle* (Colfax, La.), "Death of Col. Stubbs," May 16, 1908, 4.

7. 1860 Federal Census. *Ouachita Telegraph* (Monroe, La.), September 19, 1885, 3.

8. *Monroe News-Star* (Monroe, La.), "Monroe Fifty Years Later Soldiers Going to War," April 25, 1911, 5.

9. *New Orleans Daily Crescent*, "More Brave Louisianans in Town," April 26, 1861, 1.

10. *Monroe News Star*, April 25, 1911.

11. *New Orleans Daily Crescent*, "More Brave Louisianans in Town," April 26, 1861, 1.

12. William Watson, *Life in the Confederate Army, Being the Observations and Experiences of an Alien in the South During the American Civil War* (New York: Scribner and Welford, 1888), 139.

13. *New Orleans Crescent*, "More Brave Louisianans in Town," April 26, 1861.

14. *New Orleans Crescent*, "More Brave Louisianans in Town," April 26, 1861.

15. Robert Patrick, *Reluctant Rebel: The Secret Diary of Robert Patrick 1861–1865* (Baton Rouge: Louisiana State University Press, 1959).

16. Watson, *Life in the Confederate Army*.

17. *New Orleans Daily Crescent*, "The Metairie Camp," May 2, 1861. William Garrett Piston and Richard W. Hatcher, *Wilson's Creek: The Second Battle of the Civil War and the Men Who Fought It* (Chapel Hill: University of North Carolina Press, 2000).

18. Watson, *Life in the Confederate Army*. Patrick, *Reluctant Rebel*. Thomas W. Cutrer and T. Michael Parrish, *Brothers in Gray: The Civil War Letters of the Pierson Family* (Baton Rouge: Louisiana State University Press, 1997).

19. Camp Walker is now the Metairie Cemetery. The original ring of the racetrack was incorporated into the cemetery when it was designed after the war and is still there today.

20. Watson, *Life in the Confederate Army*.

21. Patrick, *Reluctant Rebel*.

22. Bruce S. Allardice, *More Generals in Gray* (Baton Rouge: Louisiana State University Press, 2006).

23. Watson, *Life in the Confederate Army*, 142.

24. Cutrer and Parrish, *Brothers in Gray*.

25. Patrick, *Reluctant Rebel*.

26. Watson, *Life in the Confederate Army*, 155.

27. Allardice, *More Generals in Gray*.

28. Watson, *Life in the Confederate Army*, 155.

29. Watson, *Life in the Confederate Army*, 156.

30. Author Hugh T. Harrington inspected the Edwin Jemison daguerreotype and found that it could not be removed from its frame/case without causing damage. Therefore, any identifying studio or address that may be printed on the back of the famous image must remain unknown.

31. Watson, *Life in the Confederate Army*.

32. Company designations changed throughout the war. The Pelican Grays were known at various times as Company I, F, and C. To avoid this confusion company names are used in this book.

33. *New Orleans Daily Crescent*, May 10, 1861, May 13, 1861.

34. David A. Norris, *Life During the Civil War*, Moorshead Magazines, 2009, 51.

35. An unexplained entry on the company muster roll for May 11 to June 30 listed Eddie as "absent." Under "remarks" it is stated that he is "Detached on special service under Gen. Magruder." Eddie is not the only man who is listed in such a manner. Over 100 men, from several companies of the 2nd Louisiana, have the same notation. Magruder was promoted from colonel to brigadier general on June 21, 1861, with effective date of June 17. It may be inferred that this service was in the second half of June 1861 due to the use of the rank of "general." NARA, E. F. Jemison, Service Record, June 1861.

CHAPTER THREE: FIRST BLOOD — THE PENINSULA CAMPAIGN

1. U.S. War Department, *The War of the Rebellion: A Compilation of the Official Records of the Union and Confederate Armies*, Series 1, vol. 11, chapter XIII, 405–11.

2. U.S. War Department, *The War of the Rebellion*, Series 1, vol. 9, 49–50.

3. U.S. War Department, *The War of the Rebellion*, Series 1, vol. 9, 53.

4. U.S. War Department, *The War of the Rebellion*, Series 1, vol. 9, 51.

5. U.S. War Department, *The War of the Rebellion*, Series 1, vol. 9, 57.

6. This April 5 skirmish known as "Lee's Mill" is sometimes confused with the battle at Dam No. 1 which occurred on April 16. The location of this skirmish is now covered by Lee Hall Reservoir.

7. Stephen W. Sears, *To the Gates of Richmond: The Peninsula Campaign* (New York: Ticknor & Fields, 1992), 43.

8. U.S. War Department, *The War of the Rebellion*, Series 1, vol. 11, part 1, 420–21.

9. James M. Matthews, ed., *Public Laws of the Confederate States of America, Passed at the First Session of the First Congress* (Richmond: R.M. Smith, Printer to Congress, 1862).

10. Robert Jemison, Sr., Letter to William McCullah, June 5, 1862,

Land Office, Monroe, La. State of Louisiana Administrative Division, Office of State Lands.

CHAPTER FOUR: THE DEFENSE OF RICHMOND

1. U.S. War Department, *The War of the Rebellion: A Compilation of the Official Records of the Union and Confederate Armies*, Series 1, vol. 9, chapter XXIII, 408–9.

CHAPTER FIVE: MURDER AT MALVERN HILL

1. Brig. Gen. Howell Cobb (1815–1868) was a former U.S. Congressman, governor of Georgia, and secretary of the U.S. Treasury. After secession Cobb was president of the Provisional Confederate Congress and was considered for president of the Confederacy. Prior to the war he had a plantation outside of Milledgeville. The plantation was burned by order of General Sherman in 1864. Although Cobb and Eddie had Milledgeville connections, it is highly unlikely that Cobb and Eddie had any contact prior to their military service.

2. John Brown Gordon, *Reminiscences of the Civil War* (New York: Charles Scribner's and Sons, 1904), 71.

3. Douglas Southall Freeman, *R. E. Lee: A Biography* (New York: Charles Scribner's Sons, 1935), 2:204.

4. Brig. Gen. Daniel Harvey Hill (1821–1889) was president of Middle Georgia Military and Agricultural College (now Georgia Military College) in Milledgeville from 1885 to 1889. When he would attend the annual Confederate Memorial Day ceremonies at the Confederate monument in Memory Hill Cemetery (then, City Cemetery) he would literally have walked past the monument to Eddie Jemison which mentions that he died at Malvern Hill. One wonders if he ever stopped, read the inscription, and remembered the day. General Hill's apartment in the old statehouse is visible from Eddie's memorial 540 yards away.

5. Daniel Harvey Hill, "McClellan's Change of Base, the Confederate Pursuit," *Century Illustrated Monthly Magazine*, May 1885–October 1885, vol. 30, New Series, vol. VIII, 450.

6. Brig. Gen. Ambrose Ransom Wright (1826–1872), known as "Rans," was a first cousin once removed of Edwin Jemison. They may never have met, as Wright grew up in Louisville, Ga., fifty miles east of Milledgeville. On July 13, 1862, General Wright's wife gave birth to a child they named Malvern Hill Wright.

7. Stephen W. Sears, *To the Gates of Richmond: The Peninsula Campaign* (New York: Ticknor & Fields, 1992), 325.

8. Gordon, *Reminiscences*, 74–75.

9. Tom Fort survived the war and lived in Chattanooga, Tennessee, where he was mayor in 1876, dying in 1910. On the Confederate left a few hours later Eddie's first cousin once removed, twenty-three-year-old Lt. John Stubbs, son of Peter and Ann (Hammond) Stubbs, of the 12th Georgia Regiment was advancing on the west side of Willis Church Road, preparing to attack, when orders were received to halt and not to charge.

10. Howell Cobb, August 12, 1862, report, O.R. series 1, vol. 11, part II, 748–50.

11. Capt. R. S. Williams, "Thirteenth Regiment," in *Histories of the Several Regiments and Battalions from North Carolina in the Great War 1861–1865*, ed. Walter Clark (Raleigh: State of North Carolina, E. M. Ezzell printer, 1901), 662.

12. Daniel Harvey Hill, "McClellan's Change of Base," *Century Illustrated Monthly Magazine*, May 1885–October 1885, vol. 30, New Series, vol. VII, 451–52.

13. Fitz John Porter, "The Last of the Seven Days' Battles," *Century Illustrated Monthly Magazine*, May 1885–October 1885, vol. 30, new series, vol. VIII, 625–26.

14. Casualties in the 2nd Louisiana Regiment were in the 40 percent range.

15. Julia Stubbs Pratt, Eddie's aunt, in a February 1863 letter, in Betsy Lawson Willis and James Webb Strudwick, *Genealogy and Letters of the Strudwick, Ashe, Young and Allied Families* (Alexandria, VA.: privately printed, 1971), 175–76.

16. Of the approximately 30,000 Confederates engaged at Malvern Hill, roughly 5,150 were killed or wounded and 500 went missing. The Union had about 27,000 men engaged and suffered 2,100 killed and wounded. In the Seven Days battles combined the Confederacy lost 3,478 killed, 16,261 wounded, and 875 missing. The Union lost 1,734 killed, 8,062 wounded, and 6,053 missing. Brian K. Burton, *Extraordinary Circumstances: The Seven Days Battles* (Bloomington: Indiana University Press, 2001), 357, 386.

17. William W. Averell, "With the Cavalry on the Peninsula," in *Battles and Leaders of the Civil War*, ed. Robert Underwood Johnson and Clarence Clough Buel (New York: Century Company, 1888), vol. II, part II, 432.

CHAPTER SIX: HOW DID EDDIE DIE?

1. *Southern Recorder* (Milledgeville, Ga.), August 5, 1862.

2. Betsy Lawson Willis and James Webb Strudwick, *Genealogy and Letters of the Strudwick, Ashe, Young and Allied Families* (Alexandria, Va., privately printed, 1971), 175–76.

3. *Atlanta Constitution*, March 26, 1906, 8.

4. *National Tribune* (Washington, D.C.) April 19, 1906.

5. *Macon Telegraph* (Macon, Ga.), March 16, 1906, 4.

6. Mamie Jemison Chestney, *Skeletons of the History of the Jemison and Boisfeuillet Families* (Macon: privately printed, 1964), unpaginated.

7. Warren A. Moseley, Confederate Service Record, National Archives and Record Administration.

8. Henry W. Thomas, *History of the Doles-Cook Brigade, Army of Northern Virginia, CSA* (Atlanta: Franklin Printing and Publishing Company, 1903), 170.

9. Lillian Henderson, *Roster of the Confederate Soldiers of Georgia, 1861–1865* (Hapeville, Ga.: Longina & Porter, 1964), vol. 1, 620.

10. Application for Soldiers Pension Under Act of 1910. Filed in Bibb County, Georgia, September 12, 1910. Signed by Warren A. Moseley.

11. Date of move to Georgia from Confederate Pension Application.

12. 1860 Census.

13. *Union Recorder* (Milledgeville), May 23, 1882.

14. *Union Recorder* (Milledgeville), October 17, 1882, and November 21, 1882.

15. *Atlanta Constitution*, November 23, 1883.

16. *Union Recorder* (Milledgeville), July 7, 1885.

17. *Union Recorder* (Milledgeville), August 10, 1886.

18. *Union Recorder* (Milledgeville), July 21, 1891.

19. *Atlanta Constitution*, June 17, 1892.

20. *Atlanta Constitution*, October 26, 1892.

21. *Atlanta Constitution*, February 5, 1903.

22. *Atlanta Constitution*, August 28, 1907.

23. *Union Recorder* (Milledgeville), August 1, 1893.

24. *Union Recorder* (Milledgeville), July 24, 1894.

25. *Atlanta Constitution*, July 24, 1895.

26. *Newark Daily Advocate* (Newark, Ohio), December 31, 1900.

27. The advertisement appeared in newspapers outside the South:

Daily Northwestern (Oshkosh, WI), September 23, 1904; *Trenton* (NJ) *Times*, January 20, 1905, *Iowa City Daily Press*, November 11, 1904, December 21, 1904, January 20, 1905, *Fort Wayne* (IN) *Journal Gazette*, January 22, 1905, *Sandusky* (OH) *Star*, November 12, 1904.

28. Confederate Soldier's Pension Application, 1910.

29. *Atlanta Constitution*, October 28, 1905.

30. *Atlanta Constitution*, November 10, 1905.

31. *Atlanta Constitution*, December 16, 1906.

32. *Atlanta Constitution*, June 1, 1907.

33. *Atlanta Constitution*, June 5, 1907.

34. *Atlanta Constitution*, June 11, 1907.

35. *Atlanta Constitution*, August 15, 1907.

CHAPTER SEVEN: "PEACE TO HIS ASHES"

1. East Side, Section F, Lot 26. N. Latitude: 33.07530833 W. Longitude: -83.22836919.

2. *Union Recorder* (Milledgeville), February 4, 11, and 18, 1896.

3. Thomas Artope was married to Baradell Stubbs's niece, Laura C. Stubbs.

4. Macon City Directory, 1860, 1866, 1867, 1869–70, 1872, 1878, 1880.

5. *Southern Recorder* (Milledgeville), December 3, 1861.

6. *Federal Union* (Milledgeville), March 27, 1866.

7. *Georgia Journal and Messenger* (Macon), August 13, 1862.

8. *Georgia Journal and Messenger* (Macon), August 13, 1862.

9. *Southern Recorder* (Milledgeville), August 5, 1862.

10. Betsy Lawson Willis and James Strudwick, *Genealogy and Letters of the Strudwick, Ashe, Young and Allied Families* (Alexandria, Va., privately printed, 1971), 175–76. It should be noted that Willis and Strudwick misdated the letter as February 13, 1868, when from internal evidence it clearly is 1863.

11. "Ledger" as in a ledger book. The flat surface approximately the size of the grave would be as a page where the inscription could be carved.

12. Sally (Sarah) Cantey Whitaker Allen [1865–1942] and Louis H. Andrews [1866–1944], 1938 Allen/Andrews Directory of the Cemetery. This directory is a privately published, self-copied book containing the first major indexing of Memory Hill Cemetery. It is presumed that much of the information, beyond the inscriptions on

gravestones, contained in the book was provided to its authors through first-hand experience or family members. Copies of this book may be found in the City of Milledgeville's City Engineer's Office, the Mary Vinson Library in Milledgeville, and the Baldwin County Courthouse.

13. Ground-penetrating radar survey conducted by Omega Mapping Services (Woodbury, Ga.). Maps can be found at: http://www.friendsofcems.org/MemoryHill/ and the office of the Public Works Dept., City of Milledgeville, Ga.

14. "Peace to his ashes" is a traditional blessing for a dead person. It is not implied that his "ashes" are at the monument.

15. Letter, Robert E. L. Krick to Alexandra Filipowski, November 20, 2001. Malvern Hill battlefield was not included in postwar grave relocation programs and Confederate burials in woods and not farm fields per phone discussion with Robert E. L. Krick, March 25, 2016.

NOTES ON SELECT PRINCIPAL PARTICIPANTS

1. *Union Recorder*, October 30, 1894.

2. *Macon Telegraph and Messenger*, January 18, 1879, 4.

3. United Daughters of the Confederacy, Georgia Division, Salzburger Chapter, application for Sallie Jemison Myers, daughter of Robert William Jemison. Admission: February 26, 1912.

4. *Union Recorder*, December 28, 1886.

5. *Union Recorder*, October 22, 1873.

6. *Union Recorder*, November 5, 1889.

7. *Southern Recorder*, November 21, 1871.

ACKNOWLEDGMENTS

The research for *The Boy Soldier: Edwin Jemison and the Story Behind the Most Remarkable Portrait of the Civil War* has been an ongoing project for over twenty years. Many people and many research facilities have been involved. We would like to express our deep gratitude to all those who have aided us along the way. However, we realize that some names may have become lost to us over time, and to those we apologize.

No research into Edwin Jemison would have been possible without his initial identification by Jo-Ann Aiello. We, and all who are interested in Eddie, owe her a great debt of gratitude for her marvelous work. We would like to thank Muriel M. Jackson and the staff of Middle Georgia Archives, Washington Memorial Library, Macon, Ga.; Lora Peppers of Oucahita Parish Public Library in Monroe, La.; Nancy Davis Bray, Director of Special Collections, Georgia College Library, Milledgeville, Ga.; The Georgia Historical Society, Ray and Cate Wells for their unique help; Friends of Baldwin County Cemeteries; Dr. David Wiggins; Michael Schellhammer; Ephraim Rosenbaum; Robert E. L. Krick, historian, Richmond National Battlefield Park; the staff at the Irma and Paul Milstein Division of United States History, Local History and Genealogy of the New York

Public Library; and historian and novelist Jim Littlefield for his constant support and assistance in the darkest hours. Sue Harrington deserves our great appreciation for her patience, critical eye, literary skills, and computer knowledge.

To John and Elaine Stallard very special thanks for an unforgettable memory that only they could provide.

INDEX